RACISM, EMPIRICISM

and

CRIMINAL JUSTICE

Edited by

Brian D. MacLean
Anthropology and Sociology
University of British Columbia

Dragan Milovanovic
Department of Criminal Justice
Northeastern Illinois University

$10.00

To all those persons
struggling for social justice

© **1990**   The Collective Press
Vancouver, Canada
ALL RIGHTS RESERVED

ISBN 0-9694764-0-X

Canadian Cataloguing in Publication Data

Main Entry Title:

Racism, Empiricism and Criminal Justice

> 1. Criminal Justice, Administration of — Political aspects, addresses, essays, lectures. 2. Crime and Criminals — Political aspects, addresses, essays, lectures. 3. Race and Crime — Political aspects, addresses, essays, lectures. 4. Prisons and Prisoners — Political aspects, addresses, essays, lectures.
> I. MacLean, B. D. (Brian Douglas), 1950 — . II. Milovanovic, D. (Dragan), 1950.

Printed and bound in Canada by Hignell Printing Ltd.

Cover Design, Artwork: Brian MacLean

PREFACE

At the November, 1989 meetings of the American Society of Criminology, we advanced the idea of preparing a reader on the subject of discrimination in the American Criminal Justice System as our way of helping to successfully launch the newly formed Division on Critical Criminology. The project was unanimously endorsed, and the contents of the following pages represent the product of a collective effort from a variety of individuals.

In framing the project, it was decided that we should attempt to prepare a book which was structured in such a way as to provide somewhat of an alternative to a more traditional pedagogical style. We asked the authors to prepare shorter discussion essays unconstrained by rigid academic parameters. In this way, we bring to the introductory student a set of lively debates which are readily intelligible, and which facilitate participation in classroom discussion by students and instructors alike. Given the ideological barrage of claims concerning the fairness of contemporary justice, and the heated debates which these foster, we felt that an investigation into the case both for and against discrimination would be timely.

The book is organized into three sections which fall between our introductory and concluding chapters. In Section One, noted authors debate the 'no discrimination' thesis (NDT). Wilbanks first spells out the NDT, followed by critiques from Richey Mann and Georges-Abeyie. Wilbanks then replies to the criticisms raised in these two short essays. In the three essays which follow, a methodologically-based polemic is developed by Lynch, Ansari and Georges-Abeyie. In Section Two, "Racism, Empiricism, and Policy Implications", the discrimination issue is addressed at different levels by different studies. Lynch and Patterson challenge the Wilbanks' thesis with their analysis of primary data secured from four jurisdictions. DeKeseredy and MacLean criticize Wilbanks' method, and use his own arguments to demonstrate the way in which Native criminality is constructed by the Canadian parole process. Wilbanks then comments on a recent U.S. Supreme Court decision which disallows the introduction of statistical evidence (the 'Baldus study') against the infliction of the death penalty. In the last chapter of the section, Milovanovic reacts to both Wilbanks' criticisms of the Court decision and 'reverse discrimination' decisions, identifying the latter as cases of 'repressive formalism'. Section Three serves as the synthesis section in which Headley, Zatz, French, and Danner and Landis evaluate the arguments presented in the first two sections.

We leave the final conclusions to the reader; however, the chapters in the last section, and our concluding chapter, hopefully, will serve as a guide to clarifying the issues pertaining to discrimination, and how these are to be studied.

Despite the brevity of presentation, to bring this small project to fruition in such a short period of time would not have been possible without the assistance of a number of people. This final presentation has benefitted greatly from the efforts of Celesta A. Albonetti, Dawn Currie, Marty Schwartz and Jim Thomas who all reviewed various sections of the manuscript at different stages of its completion. We should also like to thank the Division on Critical Criminology of The American Society of Criminology for providing us with the encouragement and support to undertake this project. The assistance of P. J. MacLean around the office, proved invaluable. Also, we should like to thank each of the contributors for their innovative efforts and for meeting the restrictive deadlines necessary to the timely completion of the project.

As the editors of this work, our own bias should be articulated. We argue that the criminal justice system in North American society is, perhaps, one of the most discriminatory sets of organized practices currently operant in liberal democratic social formations. As academics, we analyze this situation — as participants in the struggle for social justice, we applaud the efforts of those who struggle for dignity, equality and fairness in their treatment. May the combined efforts of all those involved in producing this book be useful to this struggle, while sensitizing the readership to the importance of a critical scrutiny of the contemporary administration of justice.

Brian D. MacLean   Dragan Milovanovic
July, 1990

TABLE OF CONTENTS

CHAPTER 1

INTRODUCTION

An Anatomy of The 'No Discrimination Thesis'

B. MacLean / D. Milovanovic

Race, gender and class biases in the criminal justice system have been observed at many levels by divergently oriented theorists employing both quantitative and qualitative research techniques. Conversely, there are a number of researchers who deny the existence of such discrimination and argue that the criminal justice system is fair. Most recently, William Wilbanks makes this claim with his 'no discrimination thesis' (NDT). As critical criminologists we want to debate this issue. With some reluctance to give undue legitimacy to these contentions, we fear that by not addressing the NDT, much of what has been gained by minorities through bitter struggles stands to be lost by the increasing mis-use of 'data' to support the notion of 'no discrimination', particularly by the courts.

While biases sometimes operate directly within the criminal justice system, at times they are 'extra-legal' in that they operate within broader society to make minorities more vulnerable to criminal justice scrutiny. Sometimes these biases are the direct result of a specific characteristic, and sometimes they are indirect in that they result from a combination of characteristics. Thus we may see the direct discriminatory effects of race on outcomes in criminal justice processing or we may find the indirect effect of race in combination with class and/or gender in these outcomes. Sometimes, discriminatory effects are overt. For example, we may find that a particular judge always sentences people of color to more severe sentences; however, sometimes the biases are covert in that the discrimination is masked by a specific set of categories. For example, we may find that people of color are less likely to receive probation as opposed to incarceration — not because they are considered to have a higher level of 'criminality', but because they are considered to have fewer community supports. The problem for academic criminology is to unravel all of these combinations in the serious attempt to grasp the extent and severity of the dispensation of unfair justice administration to the less powerful people in our society.

Discrimination also can be hidden by definition. For example, Georges-Abeyie introduces the concept of 'petit apartheid' in this book. By this he means that biases are less visible by official data alone, and often come in the forms of: harassment and insults; excessive stops, searches and questioning by police; condescending judges; narrow instructions by judges to juries; less stringent standards of evidence used in convictions of minorities, and so forth. Wilbanks has attempted to address this definitional issue in his first essay. Racism, he tells us, can be either conscious or unconscious and individual or institutional, including 'the domination of society by white culture'. He suggests that we abandon the concept 'racism' for the concepts of 'racial prejudice' which is an attitude, and 'racial discrimination' which he conceives as an act. In reply, Zatz argues that discrimination must be studied at both the overt and covert levels by both observational *and* statistical methods of analysis. Wilbanks argues against using the former, contending that observation is much too subjective and hence biased research while implying that his own quantitative methods are unbiased.

By way of sharp contrast, Danner and Landis point out that choosing a particular methodology already implicates a particular epistemology. For example, they argue that a 'feminist empiricism' can call into question many of the assumptions of positivistic methodology, indicating, for example, that a researcher's gender, race, or class standing conditions the selection of problems, the definitions to be used, the methodology to be followed, and the implications and conclusions to be drawn. Their argument in favour of greater scrutiny of researchers' assumptions can be situated within the debate concerning 'objectivity' in social sciences.

Zatz suggests that discrimination research has come in four waves: the first wave from the 1930s to the mid 1960s, indicated discrimination which was clear and consistent. The second wave from the late 1960s to the 1970s, was much more empirically sophisticated and concerned itself with controlling for relevant legal factors. Research which indicated a diminishing effect of race was countered by a refocus on the 'indirect' effects that placed minorities in situations of disadvantage. In the 1970s an 1980s, the third wave focused on the findings of the research of wave two and demonstrated that indirect effects were more important than direct effects in their impact on criminal justice decision making. Also, in the late 1970s and 1980s, the fourth wave focused more on sentencing policies, particularly those claiming to reduce discrimination by way of more sensitive standards, criteria, and rules. Here, the jury is still out. Some research substantiates direct and indirect discrimination, while other research, such as that by Wilbanks, claims that the direct effects of race result in no discrimination. The essays in this book attempt to de-construct this debate for the student. We can now turn to the first section of the book in which the extent of the debate is elaborated.

SECTION I:

DEBATES

CHAPTER 2

The Myth of a Racist Criminal Justice System

William Wilbanks
Florida International University

INTRODUCTION

White and black Americans differ sharply over whether their criminal justice system is racist. The vast majority of blacks appear to believe that the police and courts do discriminate against blacks, whereas a majority of whites reject this charge. A sizable minority of whites even believe that the justice system actually discriminates *for* blacks in "leaning over backward" for them in reaction to charges of racism from the black community and the media.

The contrasting views of blacks and whites as to the fairness of the criminal justice system are of more than academic interest as research indicates that the higher level of offending by blacks may be due in part to the belief that "the system" is unfair. This belief produces a "justification for no obligation" or the attitude that "I don't respect a system that is racist, and so I don't feel obliged to abide by the laws of that system." This view in the collective has led to riots in Miami and other cities. Furthermore, the hostility to police generated by the belief has led to a mutual expectation of violence between police and blacks that has produced more violence as part of a self-fulfilling prophecy. Finally, the white backlash to affirmative action programs may be due in part to the perception that blacks complain about racism in a society that actually practices reverse discrimination (favoritism toward blacks).

THE THESIS

I take the position that the perception of the criminal justice system as racist is a myth. This overall thesis should not be misinterpreted. I do believe that there is racial prejudice and discrimination *within* the criminal justice system, in that there are individuals, both white and black, who make decisions, at least in part, on the basis of race. I do not believe that *the system* is characterized by racial prejudice or discrimination *against* blacks. At every point from arrest to parole there is little or no evidence of an overall racial effect, in that the percentage outcomes for blacks and whites are not very different. There is evidence, however, that some individual decision makers (e.g., police officers, judges) are more likely to give 'breaks' to whites than to blacks. However, there appears to be an *equal* tendency for other individual decision-makers to favor blacks over whites. This "canceling-out effect" results in studies that find no *overall* racial effect.

The assertion that the criminal justice system is not racist does not address the reasons why blacks appear to offend at higher rates than whites before coming into contact with the criminal justice system. It may be that racial discrimination in American society has been responsible for conditions (e.g., discrimination in employment, housing, and education) that lead to higher rates of offending by blacks, but that possibility does not bear on the question of whether the criminal justice system discriminates against blacks. Also, the thesis that racism *is* not systematic and pervasive in the criminal justice system does not deny that racial prejudice and discrimination have existed or have even been the dominant force in the design and operation of the criminal justice system in the past.

DEFINING RACISM

One of the main barriers to the discussion and resolution of the issue of racism in the criminal justice system involves the multiple uses and meanings of the term 'racism'. Definitions of this term range from a conscious attitude by an individual to an unconscious act by an institution or even to the domination of society by white culture. I have suggested that the term 'racism' be abondoned in favor of the terms 'racial prejudice' (an attitude) and 'racial discrimination' (an act).

Any discussion of the pervasiveness of racism in the criminal justice system is clouded by the tendency of accusers (e.g., those who claim the system is racist) to use a double standard in that the term is used only to apply to whites. For example, it is often pointed out that 50% of the victims of police killings are black and that this fact alone presents a prima facie case of racism. But it is seldom pointed out that 50% of the police officers who are killed are victimized by blacks. If the first fact indicates racism by white police officers why does not the second fact indicate racism by black killers of police?

At times the use of the term racism appears to constitute a 'non-falsifiable thesis' in that any result is defined as racist. For example, in *McCleskey* v. *Georgia* (see attendant article) the petitioner claims that he received the death penalty because he (a black) killed a white whereas those who kill blacks seldom receive the death penalty. Thus lenient treatment given to black killers (or those who kill black victims) is defined as racism. But if black killers had been more likely to be sentenced to death that result would also be (and has been) viewed as racist. Thus the term is defined so that any result is indicative of

6

racism (*i.e.*, a non-falsifiable thesis). The double standard of racism is also seen in this case in that the death penalty statistics actually indicate harsher treatment of white than black killers but this result is not seen as racism (against whites).

In a similar fashion a lower percentage of blacks (than whites) being convicted has been interpreted by accusers as racist in that this result indicates that charges against blacks were often without substance. On the other hand, if more blacks were convicted this result would also be viewed by accusers as being indicative of racism, since black defendants were treated more harshly.

THE DATA

The book was under-taken to explain why blacks in the U.S. are 8 times more likely, on a *per capita* basis, to be in prison than are whites. The major point of the book is that the approximate 8:1 *per capita* ratio of blacks to whites in prison is the result of an approximate 8:1 level in offending and not the result of racial selectivity by the police and the courts. In other words, the 8:1 black to white ratio at offending is not increased as offenders are brought into and processed by the criminal justice system.

Some original data is presented in an appendix to the book on the black *vs.* white gap from arrest to incarceration in prison for two states—California and Pennsylvania. In 1980 felony cases, blacks in California were arrested 5.2 times as often as whites. This black/white gap increased to 6.2% at incarceration. Thus the black/white 'gap' increased by 20% from arrest to prison. However, the reverse occurred in Pennsylvania where the 8.1% gap at arrest decreased to 7.4 at incarceration (a decline of 9%). Overall, it would appear that the black/white gap does not increase from arrest to prison. Thus there is no evidence overall that black offenders processed by the criminal justice system fare worse than white offenders.

But perhaps the black/white gap at arrest is a product of racial bias by the police in that the police are more likely to select and arrest black than white offenders. The best evidence on this question comes from the National Crime Survey which interviews 130,000 Americans each year about crime victimization. Those who are victimized by violent crime are asked to describe the offenders (who were not necessarily caught by the police) as to age, sex and race. The percent of offenders described by victims as being black is generally consistent with the percent of offenders who are black according to arrest figures. For example, approximately 60% of (uncaught) robbers described by victims were black and approximately 60% of those arrested for robbery in the U.S. are black. This would not be the case if the police were 'picking on' black robbers and ignoring white robbers.

Given the above figures, those who claim that racism is systematic and pervasive in the criminal justice system should explain why the black/white gap does not cumulatively increase from arrest to prison. Furthermore, those who claim racism is pervasive should be asked to specify the number of black offenders that are thought to receive harsher treatment (e.g., whether 10%, 50% or 100%) and the extent of that 'extra' harshness in cases where 'it' is given. For example, at sentencing do those mistreated black offenders receive on the average a 10%, 50% or 100% harsher sentence?

There is a large body of research on the alleged existence of racial discrimination at such points as arrest, conviction and sentencing. The bibliography of my book lists over 80 sentencing studies which examined the impact of race on outcome. A number of scholars have examined this large body of research and concluded that there is no evidence of systematic racial discrimination. James Q. Wilson, the most prominent American criminologist, asserts that the claim of discrimination is not supported by the evidence as did a three volume study of the sentencing literature by the National Academy of Sciences.

METHODOLOGICAL PROBLEMS

Some studies do claim to have found evidence of racial discrimination. However, as Wilson and others have pointed out, most of these studies are marked by flaws in design or interpretation. One chapter of *The Myth of a Racist Criminal Justice System* is devoted to seven models of design and/or interpretation which have been utilized in studies of the possible existence of racial discrimination. Many of the studies claiming to have found racial discrimination utilized a model of analysis that ensured such a result.

But many readers will be thinking at this point that "one can prove anything with statistics" and thus that the validity of the claim for a racist criminal justice system should be determined by what one knows by personal experience or observation. However, the layperson's confidence in and reliance upon 'common-sense' in rejecting the statistical approach to knowledge in favor of what one knows by personal experience and observation is misplaced. The layperson does not take into account the impact of bias (and in some cases racial prejudice) in personal experience and observation.

Let us take, for example, the question as to whether there is racial discrimination in the use of force by the police. Those who reject studies of large numbers of 'use of force' incidents which do not show evidence of racial discrimination by race of victim suggest that 'unbiased' observation will reveal racism. But suppose that several people see a white police officer hit a black youth. There are a multitude of explanations (e.g., the youth hit the officer first, the youth resisted authority, the officer was the macho type who would hit any victim who was not properly deferential, the officer was a racist) for such an act. The tendency is for those with a particular bias to select that explanation which is consistent with their bias. For example, other police officers or white citizens might select the explanation that the youth resisted authority while black citizens might select the explanation that the officer was a racist. In either case, the observer simply infers the explanation that is most consistent with his/her bias, and thus knowledge via observation is anything but unbiased. Large-scale statistical studies allow one to control for factors (other than race) which might impact on a decision or act. Without such studies those who disagree on the impact of racism will simply be trading anecdotal ("I know a case where...") to 'prove' their case.

CONCLUSION

Racial prejudice, in my view, is the process by which people assign positive traits and motives to themselves and their race and negative traits and motives to 'them' (the other race). Blacks tend to see the beating of a black youth by a white police officer as being indicative of racism (an evil motive or trait attributed to the 'out-group') while whites (or police officers) tend to see the beating as being the result of some improper action by the black youth. The white view is also influenced by the assigning of evil motives or traits to the out-group (to the black youth). In both cases the observers, whether black or white, have been influenced by racial prejudice in their assigning of blame or cause for the incident.

My basic position is that both the black and white views on the extent of racism in the criminal justice system are 'ignorant' in that personal knowledge is gained primarily via observation and experience — methods which are heavily influenced by bias and racial prejudice. In other words, racial prejudice keeps the races polarized on this issue since each race sees the 'facts' which 'prove' its thesis. Statistical studies of large numbers of blacks and whites subjected to a particular decision (e.g., the use of force) are a safeguard against personal bias and are far more valid as a means to 'truth' than personal observation and experience. It is my view that an examination of those studies available at various points in the criminal justice system fails to support the view that racial discrimination is pervasive. It is in this sense that the belief in a racist criminal justice is a myth.

The Myth of a Racist Criminal Justice System examines all the available studies that have examined the possible existence of racial discrimination from arrest to parole. For example, the chapter on the police examines the evidence for and against the charge that police deployment patterns, arrest statistics, the use of force ('brutality') and the use of deadly force reflect racism. The chapter on the prosecutor examines the evidence for and against the charge that the bail decision, the charge, plea bargaining, the provision of legal counsel, and jury selection are indicative of racism. The chapter on prison looks at evidence concerning the possibility of racism as reflected through imprisonment rates for blacks *vs.* whites, in racial segregation, in treatment programs, in prison discipline and in the parole decision. In general, this examination of the available evidence indicates that support for the 'discrimination thesis' is sparse, inconsistent, and frequently contradictory.

CHAPTER 3

The Myth of a Racist Criminal Justice System ?

Daniel Georges-Abeyie
Florida State University

Wilbanks' book is an important work not because it presents heretofore unknown data and unique theoretical analyses of 'black' criminality and the criminal justice "system" processing of 'black' 'offenders', for it does not. It is important for its revival of the Michael J. Hindelang Thesis, *i.e.*, the reality of black crime propensity as denoted by an alleged value free empiricism. It is also important for its bold utilization of consensus theory and selective reverse labeling theory, logic, and analysis.

Wilbanks contends that the punitively differential treatment of blacks via the U.S criminal justice system is a myth, a residual belief borne of an earlier era when Negroid racial identity was, or may have been, a decisive factor in the treatment of the alleged 'black' offender. He contends that if differential treatment of blacks does occur via the criminal justice system, the discrimination is in the direction of greater leniency. He also contends that blacks are more 'racially prejudiced' than whites, victimize whites more often than whites victimize blacks, and that the black targeting of white victims involves more than chance. His rejection of what he labels the discrimination thesis (*i.e.*, the actualization of systematic, systemic bias) is based upon his analysis of systematic racial bias in the formal decision making process of the U.S. criminal justice 'system'. Wilbanks contends that: (1) the criminal justice system has been plagued by a failure to agree on a definition of racism; (2) black decision-makers may not make a difference, much less a positive difference, with respect to the treatment of blacks processed by the 'system'; (3) "if the Discrimination Thesis (DT) is valid and racial disproportionality indicates racism, why is the black/white incarceration gap lowest in the southern states, where prejudice is allegedly greatest and highest in some states where prejudice is allegedly less extensive?" and (4) "[that] if the DT is valid, if blacks are more likely to be punished for attacking whites and if whites are less likely to be punished for attacking blacks, why do black offenders choose white victims more frequently than black victims?"

Reprinted with permission from *The Critical Criminologist* Vol. 1, No. 3, Summer, 1989

There are numerous analytical as well as theoretical issues raised by Wilbanks' thesis noted above. Does the focus of criminal justice analysis on the formal, easily observed decision-making process obscure or even misdirect attention from the most significant contemporary form of racism within the criminal justice system? e.g., the everyday insults, rough or brutal treatment, and unnecessary stops, questions, and searches of blacks; the lack of civility faced by black suspects/arrestees; the quality, clarity, and objectivity of the judges' instructions to the jury when a black arrestee is on trial; the acceptance of lesser standards of evidence in cases that result in the conviction of black arrestees, as well as numerous other punitively discretionary acts by law enforcement and correctional officers as well as jurists. These are the punitively discriminatory, discretionary acts this reviewer has labeled 'petit apartheid', discriminatory behavior not analyzed by Wilbanks. The decision to focus on easily observed data, *i.e.*, the most inflammatory anecdotal references and statistical data excludes much while including a limited sample of criminal justice facts. The aggregation of 'free world' offender data with offenses committed by black convicts and/or detainees against white and non-white inmates and detainees inevitably results in conclusions that have merged very different crime-perpetuation/crime-victimization dynamics; dynamics that include close residential proximity in correctional and detention facilities (even forced tier block integration) with rigid patterns of expanding 'free world' residential spatial segregation. If one does explore official crime statistics, why were capital punishment statistics on sentence commutation given short thrift? Is there a racial or ethnic bias manifested in the assignment of level of security/custody in correctional as well as detention facilities?

As for Wilbanks' contention that blacks are more prejudiced than whites, there is no sound statistical proof of this contention but even if such data did exist the significant issue remains, "Are blacks more *racist* than whites ?", not whether they are more 'prejudiced'. Blacks for the most part lack the socio-political-economic power relationship to transform their prejudice (attitudes/beliefs) into racism (*i.e.*, behavior that subordinates someone, in this case a white, because of his/her race or characteristics attributed to race). The contention that the black/white incarceration gap is lowest in the southern states where prejudice is allegedly greatest and highest in some states where prejudice is allegedly less extensive lacks statistical support in regard to the extent of black/white prejudice (attitudes and beliefs) much less racism (behavior). The incarceration gap may reflect a demographic reality geographers and social ecologists have explored in the concept of 'threat ratio or tipping point', *i.e.*, whites might feel most threatened by those people with whom they have limited secondary much less primary relations. Thus, whites, in states with relatively limited black populations, may be especially severe with black alleged offenders especially where the primary knowledge of blacks in general is gleaned from the evening news and mass consumption cinema in which the imagery of blacks as deviates and predators is sustained.

Similar to the late Michael J. Hindelang, Wilbanks equates race with ethnicity and thus lacks an analysis that notes differential rates of black ethnic criminality as well as criminal victimization. Thus, ethnically diverse blacks are treated as one ethnic group. His analysis, similar to the Hindelang analysis, also lacks a spatial sophistication that might be cognizant of racial and ethnic bias by jurors and judges when crimes occur within specific ecological zones of the alleged ghetto, slum-ghetto, or non-ghetto.

The statement that there is no evidence that supports the contention that black criminal justice practitioners make a difference in the treatment of blacks is interesting but myopic in terms of analysis. The lack of differential treatment of black suspects, arrestees, and convicted felons might merely manifest the reality of a Eurocentric criminal justice practitioner selection process that excludes the most obviously black-oriented candidates.

The reliance upon official criminal justice offender and victimization data in order to contend that black assailants, rapists, and robbers more frequently choose white than black victims is a fallacious conclusion. This conclusion is probably the result of the under-reporting of intraracial F.B.I. Part-One offenses by blacks combined with a profound ignorance of the spatial dynamics of black residential patterns and black intraracial crime perpetration. An example of the latter is that assault and rape charges are often initiated by health care professionals, rather than by black victims, if the offense occurred within the slum-ghetto environment.

The Wilbanks contention that "if DT is valid, how does one explain why many studies have found that blacks receive more lenient treatment than whites at a particular point for a particular crime?" is characteristic of the misdirections so much a part of the Wilbanks thesis. The question misdirects attention but is readily answered. The leniency of sentence for a black arrestee charged with the victimization of a black may reflect a societal (or jurist) perception of the limited worth of a black's life, property, or person. Such leniency may be the crystallization of prejudicial attitudes/beliefs in the form of racist action, not a statement of the rejection of racism.

In summary, the Wilbanks thesis is not grounded in the experiential reality of 'why' and 'how' black-on-black offenses go either un-reported or under-reported. He ignores the reality of a Eurocentric selection process in the employment of black criminal justice practitioners. He confuses black prejudice for racism, ignores the spatial dynamic, aggregates 'free world' and corrections/detention statistics, equates black racial identity with ethnicity, and ignores significant 'petit apartheid' criminal justice realities while fixating upon easily observed discriminatory practices, limited aggregated statistical data, and inflammatory anecdotal references in order to reject a rigidly defined and unrealistic 'Discrimination Thesis'. As for why black predators rob whites? Whites have money and other items of worth. The selection of white robbery victims may have nothing to do with prejudice but everything to do with socio-economic class and the distribution of wealth in this capitalist society.

CHAPTER 4

Random Thoughts On The Ongoing Wilbanks-Mann Discourse

Coramae Richey Mann

Indiana University

My continuing dialogue with Florida International University's Bill Wilbanks as to whether the criminal justice system is racist or not is slowly taking on the character of a "dog and pony show" which a bit of history (herstory?) should clarify. In 1987 Brooks-Cole released Wilbanks' controversial book, *The Myth of a Racist Criminal Justice System*. A shocked reaction, particularly among critical criminologists, was immediate and Trey Williams requested me to respond to Willbanks' book and asked Wilbanks to reiterate his position; thus, presenting both sides of the question in an issue of the *Criminal Justice Research Bulletin*. In 1988, Wilbanks and I were invited to debate at the national meetings of the American Criminology Association in Chicago. Our next "appearance" is at the invitation of Ralph Weisheit in April for the Annual Spring Conference of the Department of Criminal Justice, the Criminal Justice Association at Illinois State University, entitled "Racism and Criminal Justice: Myths and Realities." Contrary to how it appears, I am not trying to make a career out of this (the "dog and pony show" reference) but I do feel compelled to continue the dialogue, especially in the light of recent events concerning the topic.

For example, in Chicago, one of my former Ph.D. students in the ASC debate audience commented that he felt that several people around him appeared to agree with the Wilbanks thesis. Apparently they were mumbling and commenting among themselves but did not speak out. This type of non-action scares me for two reasons: (1) they were criminology colleagues who felt as Wilbanks did and (2) they did not articulate their feelings in the provided open forum. In either instance, there was no way to attempt to persuade them that the criminal justice system is racist. I am fearful of the

Reprinted with permission from *The Critical Criminologist* Vol. 1, No. 3, Summer, 1989 thoughts festering in them and the nature and content of their instruction to students and colleagues that stem from those thoughts.

A second incident is more frustrating. As a part of the Indiana University Black History Month program in February, I was a member of a panel on the roles of blacks in criminal justice. Since one of the panelists could not appear, the two of us remaining barely avoided a debate. The other panelist was a former black police officer and correction officer. In his opening remarks he stated that as a result of his employment experiences he had changed his opinion about blacks in the criminal justice system: he was now pro-capital punishment and he felt that black offenders made the choice to be criminal and should be punished severely. He also felt that he and other police and correction officers were the real 'brothers', and upon my probing, agreed that his was the 'us' against 'them' position typical of law enforcement and corrections personnel.

Both the ASC non-verbalizing colleagues and the extremely vocal black colleagues at Indiana University represent an undercurrent of opinion that is as problematic as Bill Wilbanks' book — they border on the dangerous and clearly represent the paucity of humanness permeating the United States today and the concomitant emergence of the once subtle and underground racism pervasive in this nation. One of the statements in my paper that I did not make in Chicago was that Wilbanks' book "is replete with so many innuendoes and untruths that the unaware reader, in accepting these statements as fact, may become as anti-black or anti-minority as readers of *Mein Kampf* became anti-Semitic. And I need not emphasize the horror that led to."

Wilbanks admits there was once racism in the criminal justice system, but while today there may be a few bad apples in the system, the whole barrel isn't rotten. My position is that the racism in the criminal justice system has become institutionalized in the same way that it has in other organizational segments of the nation such as education, politics, religion, and the economic structure; and the barrel *is* rotten. I am far from alone in this belief; a national survey last year reported that a majority of Americans state that our society remains racist and four out of ten respondents believed that racial equality would not occur in their lifetimes. There are other notable facts to consider. Almost all of our cities (96.4%) are racially segregated. A former Ku Klux Klan Grand Dragon was just elected a state representative in Louisiana. The National Council of Churches last year deplored "a national epidemic of hate-motivated violence against a growing variety of minority groups..." Research funded by the National Institute of Justice, currently underway in New York City and

Baltimore County concerns such biased-based violence and Jim Garafalo's preliminary findings suggest what many people of color have known for most of their lives — minorities are targets of hatred and violent acts simply because of their skin color.

These are not isolated incidents but are mentioned to highlight only a small part of the very large problem of racism in this country. If the country is plagued with racism, I ask Wilbanks: how, according to his own admission, can the historically racist criminal justice system be exempt ? Wilbanks ignores that question as well as the larger issue of racism in the criminal justice system and instead focuses on the alleged disproportionate criminality among blacks. It is true that while black Americans are about 12% of the U.S. population they account for about 30% of arrests, 41% of those in jails, 45% in prisons, 30% on probation or parole, and 40% currently on the death rows in the states of this nation. Wilbanks incites racism through the reporting of similar figures while simultaneously ignoring the fact that blacks are *not* more criminal than any other racial/ethnic subgroup in this country.

The usual way that F.B.I. Uniform Crime Report arrest statistics are compared is *across* racial groups. I will demonstrate in my next book, *Minorities, Crime, and Public Policy*, that an examination of arrest statistics *within* each subgroup, instead of *between* subgroups, produces a totally different picture — one that reveals no significant racial differences between types of crime or extent of crime. In this analysis I examined 1986 UCR data, since this was the last year that Hispanic Americans were included as an identifiable group. From this internal examination, among index crimes, only 7.7% of blacks' arrests were for violent crimes and 18.4% were for property crimes, while the other 73.9% of arrests were for less serious, non-index crimes. Put another way, 26.1% of black arrests in 1986 were for index, or serious crimes. Proportions for the other subgroups are comparable: Asian Americans — 26.1%, Hispanic Americans — 21.3%, Native Americans — 19.4%, and whites — 18.9%. Further, the most frequent arrest offense for all groups was larceny-theft, the second most frequent was aggravated assault for blacks, and burglary for the other subgroups, and the third most frequent was burglary for blacks and aggravated assault for the other four subgroups. Obviously each of the racial/ethnic groups are highly similar in their criminal activities as reflected in these arrest statistics.

Given the close correspondence of arrest offenses among these minority subgroups and whites, other reasons that appear to be related to institutionalized racism apparently account for the disproportionate involvement of blacks in every tier of the criminal justice system. The 'black shift phenomenon', identified in a Washington, D.C. study, revealed increased involvement of blacks from arrest to incarceration, and decreased involvement of whites progressing through the same system.

At the law enforcement level, there is differential processing of black and white suspects. Whereas Wilbanks focuses on the formal decision making process, he ignores the informal aspects of the criminal justice process. According to Daniel Georges-Abeyie, Wilbanks overlooks the 'petit apartheid realities' in, for example, the stop-and-question and stop-and-frisk practices of the police. Numerous studies of police-minority relations identify the rudeness, insults, lack of understanding, posturing and brutality that police officers exhibit toward blacks and other minorities. A response to such demeaning behavior is quickly suppressed through arrest. Joan Petersilia and her colleagues in the Rand Inmate study found that, contrary to Wilbanks' notion that the system was lenient toward blacks, the reason that many blacks are not convicted after arrest is due to the false charges leveled against them by the police which contributed to their entry into the system in the first place.

This initial source of ingress into the criminal justice system is only the beginning of what Georges-Abeyie calls "a disjointed series of processes" fraught with institutionalized racism. Poor defendants, meaning mostly blacks, have difficulty making bail and are consequently detained in jail until their trials. This condition prevents them from assisting in securing evidence in their own defense, often results in the loss of a job if there is one, and offers a judge or jury a potentially negative visual impression of a shackled, possibly unshaven defendant in jail garb which often has the word 'prisoner' on the back. No matter how objective one may be, such a visage may influence juridical decisions, particularly if the victim is white. Once sentenced for a crime, according to U.S. Department of Justice statistics (1987), blacks typically serve more time than whites for the same offenses.

Although, like whites, blacks more frequently assault, rape, and kill members of their own kind, Darnell Hawkins accurately notes that black life is devalued by the criminal justice system. Intra-racial crimes are treated far more leniently by the courts than inter-racial crimes, especially when blacks are the perpetrators and whites are the victims. This gross racial disparity is probably most evident in cases of capital punishment. According to the NAACP Legal Defense and Educational Fund, since the reinstitution of capital punishment in 1976, not a single white defendant has been executed for killing a minority person. Further, despite Wilbanks' suggestion of 'subtle bias' and 'flaws' in the Baldus methodology, with all conventional controls held constant the slayers of white victims were still four times more likely to be assigned the death penalty than those who killed blacks — a finding contrary to the 1987 U.S. Supreme Court *McClesky* decision of no racial bias in death sentencing.

In his review of Wilbanks' book, George-Abeyie sums up the major Wilbanks' error of viewing institutionalized racism in the criminal justice system as a 'myth' by stating, "it is flawed by the *selective* presentation of data and the *selective* utilization of research findings, ideological statements, and interpretations of "fact', as well as by the basic *consensus* theory and selective *reverse* labeling theory logic of its analysis, including the questions asked or omitted." While I have produced studies on the other side of the issue, I admit that there are insufficient studies to 'prove' anything in criminology/criminal justice. As basically a qualitative researcher, and as a minority, I have studied, witnessed and personally experienced racism in the criminal justice system. In his preference for "statistical studies of large numbers of blacks and whites subjected to a particular decision", Wilbanks discounts both qualitative, observational research and minority personal experiences as 'ignorant' and invalid measures to study racism in the system. Thus we arrive at the primary disagreement in our persistent dialogue: I can accept Wilbanks' research methods if and when they are buttressed by observational, ethnographic, anecdotal, and other qualitative data; but, by stubbornly maintaining his myopic research perspective, Wilbanks effectively avoids undertaking the sorely needed in-depth study of racism in the criminal justice system.

CHAPTER 5

Response to The Critics of The Myth of a Racist Criminal Justice System

William Wilbanks
Florida International University

I hope that those who have read the two previous commentaries of *The Myth of a Racist Criminal Justice System* by Daniel Georges-Abeyie and Coramae Richey Mann will read the more objective review of the book by John Hagen in his review essay in *Criminology* (1987, May, pp. 422-28). Hagan reviews *The Myth of a Racist Criminal Justice System, Racial Disparities in the Criminal Justice System* by Joan Petersilia and *The Social Contexts of Criminal Sentencing* by Martha A. Myers and Susette Talarico and states that all three studies found only a small race effect across decision points of the criminal justice system and/or that the (small) race effect against blacks was counterbalanced by a comparable race effect for blacks. Thus a more neutral reviewer seems to agree that there is no evidence of a sizable or systematic race effect across the criminal justice system in the three most recent and comprehensive studies.

Georges-Abeyie chooses not to confront the evidence for the lack of a sizable race effect across the criminal justice system in formal decisions (arrest, sentencing, etc.) and instead suggests that racism would be readily found in less visible informal acts (which he calls 'petit apartheid') such as insults, lack of civility, etc. I concentrated on the formal decisions in my review since the claims of racism in criminal justice by Georges-Abeyie, Mann and others most often refer to such formal decisions, and since there is little empirical research to review on the more informal acts. And if there is as much racism reflected in decisions by police, jurists, etc., as he claims, why does the race gap (for formal decisions) not increase across decision points of the criminal justice system?

Georges-Abeyie also suggests that I make little mention of capital punishment statistics that suggest racism. I do regret that I did not devote more attention to this subject and have done so in later publications (e.g "Reaction to *McCleskey* vs. *Georgia*" reprinted in chapter 11 of this volume). It should be noted that the Baldus study presented to the U.S. Supreme Court in support of *McCleskey* v. *Georgia* found that the race gap (by race of victim) in Georgia was reduced to less than statistical significance after *some* controls — but not those deemed most important by prosecutors — were utilized.

Both the Georges-Abeyie and Mann reviews claim that there is no solid evidence for the viewpoint that crime rates are significantly higher for blacks than for whites. Would they deny that homicide rates are more than 500% higher for blacks than whites? And if that is the case why would anyone think that the race gaps for offending for other violent crimes (which are correlated with homicide) are not equally as great as victimization data suggest?

Georges-Abeyie and Mann seem to want to have it both ways — they want to argue that black crime is not significantly higher than white crime but then turn around and claim that the (higher?) black crime rate is a product of racial discrimination. How can it be if (as they claim) it is no higher than the white rate? Then how would they explain the (allegedly equal) white rate?

Georges-Abeyie also seems to agree that black cops (judges, etc.) do not make a difference (*i.e.*, do not reduce the race gap) but suggests that the black practitioners have sold out to the white establishment and are not acting black. I wonder if he has informed black practitioners of this conclusion? It seems that this contention is an insult to all blacks working in the criminal justice system who are trying (but failing — according to Georges-Abeyie — because they are not 'black' enough) to make a difference.

I was shocked at Georges-Abeyie's comments on my data in the book suggesting that black offenders are more likely to choose white than black victims. He clearly has not read my comments in *The Myth of a Racist Criminal Justice System* or in the original study (*Crime and Delinquency*, January, 1985) as the study was based on victimization data while his comments (as to FBI data and failure to charge, etc.) suggest that he thought I utilized police data. It seems to me that a critic should read the studies he intends to criticize.

The only person to challenge (in print) my inter-racial thesis (e.g., that black offenders are more likely to choose white, not black victims) concedes that black offenders are more likely to choose white victims but suggests that such a choice pattern is to be expected given the black/white population differences and offense rates (see: *American Journal of Sociology*, 1987, 92(4), pp. 817-35).

Coramae Mann's comments in this review and in past debates have dealt less with the case that I present and more with charges that my book is inflammatory in that it incites hatred toward blacks and is akin to *Mein Kampf*. Like Georges-Abeyie, she does not point to studies that contradict my conclusions that the race gap does not increase across decision-points of the criminal justice system. Instead she points to public opinion, racist incidents, etc., which have nothing to do with my thesis.

Mann claims that blacks do not offend at a higher rate than whites and that this 'fact' is proven by examining arrest percentages by crime within racial groups. I thought that anyone who claimed to understand statistics knew the difference between rates between groups and similarity of patterns of crime across groups but evidently this point has escaped her. I suppose she would also argue that since male and female juveniles have a similar pattern of offending that their rates of offending are similar. Likewise, I suppose she would claim that if the elderly have a similar pattern of offending to the young then their rates are similar. Frankly, I find this line of 'proof' woefully ignorant and I would be amazed if any reputable publisher would publish such a fatuous argument. Perhaps one of Mann's supporters will explain to her the difference between patterns and rates before she further embarrasses her cause.

In the above review — and in our written and oral debates — Mann has often tried to dismiss statistical evidence (of no cumulative increase in the racial gap across the criminal justice system) from *The Myth of a Racist Criminal Justice System* by suggesting that more qualitative or observational study would confirm her thesis of a racist criminal justice system. Evidently she would credit all observations of extensive racism by her and her supporters and dismiss all observations to the contrary as being conducted by biased observers. I fail to see how anyone can claim that statistical evidence is more subject to bias than observations. And I would note that Mann attempts to use statistics (e.g., death penalty research) herself when she thinks they support her cause.

Mann, like Georges-Abeyie, also misinterprets Petersilia's work. I would suggest that she read Petersilia's latest report, *Racial Equity in Sentencing* (1988) and Hagan's review of her 1983 book. It appears that more objective reviewers have seen her work as supporting my thesis rather than as contradicting it.

It is unfortunate that Georges-Abeyie and Mann have failed to address the central thesis of my book and to suggest specific studies that I have ignored or misinterpreted that would invalidate my thesis. I look forward to the publication of Mann's book. I am more than willing to let readers of both books judge which is the most objective survey of the existing evidence on the extent of racism in the criminal justice system.

CHAPTER 6

Criminal Justice Processing of Non-White Minorities

Daniel E. Georges-Abeyie
Florida State University

Daniel E. Georges-Abeyie
Florida State University

INTRODUCTION

According to federal and state criminal justice statistics, non-white criminality in general, and 'black' criminality in particular are realities of the 1980s and 90s.[1] Nevertheless, very few comprehensive texts devoted exclusively to minority crime in general, or black crime in particular, have been published during the 1980s. Perhaps, Wilbanks' *The Myth of a Racist Criminal Justice System* (1987) has been the most controversial discussion of 'race and crime' published during this period. Despite staunch theoretical, statistical, and anecdotal rebuttals [2], the Hindelang-Wilbanks thesis persists, a thesis which embodies the mythology of an objective, quantifiable analysis of black crime and criminal justice processing of blacks. This persistence has been given credence by the earnest attempt to establish sentencing guidelines while limiting judicial and law enforcement discretion.[3] For a case in point, Petersilia's 1983 study noted the following:

1. Minority suspects were more likely to be released after arrest; however, after a felony conviction, minority offenders were more likely than whites to be given longer sentences and to be put in prison instead of jails;

2. In certain states, racial differences in post sentencing treatment existed in the form and length of sentence served;

3. High post-arrest release rates for minorities do not indicate that police over-arrest minorities in proportion to the kind and amount of crime they actually commit;

4. There are some evident racial differences in criminal motivation, weapons use, and prison behavior, but most are not statistically significant;

5. Racial differences in plea bargaining and jury trials may explain some of the differences in length and type of sentence [received by blacks and whites]. Petersilia's 1988 study challenged the claim that sentencing and parole reform based on certain guidelines discriminated against blacks. She found that key predictors associated with crime upon which guidelines are based are more prevalent among blacks than among whites, and concluded that racial disparity, not discrimination is the result. (Georges-Abeyie, 1989: 36)

As will be argued below, Wilbanks' book serves as a good example of an attempt to objectify the social scientific review of data pertaining to black criminality and the criminal justice system. In chapter three, I argued that his study is critically flawed because while he purports to examine the reality, mythology, and ideology of alleged systematic racial bias in the formal decision making process of the U.S. criminal justice system, his analyis consists of: the selective presentation of data, the selective utilization of his findings, unfounded ideological statements, and interpretation of 'fact'. In addition, the analysis is biased by a commitment to basic consensus theory and selective reverse labeling theory logic evident in the questions which he either raises or ignores. In the discussion which follows, I shall examine what I consider to be seven fatal flaws in the conclusions which Wilbanks offers to his work.

CRITIQUE OF WILBANKS' SELECTIVE CONCLUSIONS
Point One

Wilbanks contends that the criminal justice system has been plagued by an inexusable failure, both by lay persons and scholars, to agree upon a definition of racism. Wilbanks is correct. Criminal justice research into the significance of racism has failed to address the general definitional issues of racism and prejudice, much less the specific definitional issues of overt and institutional racism. However, criminal justice and criminological research has not only failed to address the difference between race and ethnic diversity (much less to understand this crucial difference), but it has also ignored the equally complex issues of racism and prejudice. Wilbanks must be commended for his astute and righteous annoyance in regard to faulty theoretical premises that explore and analyze the extent and nature of racism and prejudice within the U.S. criminal justice system without first fully defining these phenomena. However, Wilbanks' definitions of (overt) racism and institutional racism merit critical comment as does his utilization of these terms to refute the discrimination thesis (DT).

Prejudice is an *attitude* not a behavior. Wilbanks' desire to be consistent by utilizing prejudice to refer to an attitude and the term discrimination to describe a *behavior* is commendable. However, the use of the term 'prejudice' to describe an attitude and 'racism' to describe a behavior is not novel. For years, social scientists have used the term racism to describe a behavior that subordinates another person. This subordination is due to race, color or some other characteristic allegedly associated with a particular racial category regardless of the intent of the subordinator (see Georges-Abeyie, 1974; Downs, 1976; Parrillo, 1985; Schaeffer, 1984). Wilbanks' contention is that if one defines racial prejudice "as the attribution of negative traits and motives to other ethnic or racial groups. . . [then] blacks are more racially prejudiced than whites". He also goes on to say that "In recent years the negative attribution process (prejudice) has decreased among whites but increased among blacks". This contention must be seriously questioned. The extent to which black prejudice has increased and white prejudice decreased is highly debatable. *The Gallup Report* (arguably liberal), *Public Opinion Poll* (American Enterprise Institute Polls, arguably extremely conservative), *Opinion Magazine*, and the various mass media opinion polls vary considerably in regard to this issue. However, when one speaks of general attitudes, beliefs, specific valuations and subsequent action one must realize that one is speaking of very different phenomena, and that the Wilbanks' approach is not cognizant of this differentiation between avowed belief and subsequent action.

The differentiation between avowed general valuations and specific evaluations was first noted and analyzed by Frank R. Westie. Westie (1965) addressed this issue of variance between general valuations (generally spoken and 'advertised' beliefs) and specific valuations (the application of such general assertions as brotherhood, equality, freedom of choice) in situations involving blacks. To the duality noted by Westie, one must add the issue of the actualization of the specific valuation, i.e., *behavior*. Thus, one can state that all persons are equal and that prejudice and racism are wrong (general valuations). One might view assault as an evil, a wrong to be condemned and prosecuted (a general valuation). Nonetheless, one might view black assault upon a white differently than a black assault upon a black (specific valuations), or a white assault upon a white, or even a white assault upon a black (another specific valuation). Thus a more severe sentence may be applied to a black assailant of a white victim than to a black assailant of a black victim, or to a white assailant of a black victim, or to a white assailant of a white victim (the actualization of the specific valuation).

As noted in general and specific valuation statements, white racial prejudices (attitudes) may have possibly decreased while black prejudicial attitudes may have increased. At the same time, however, the actualization of the specific valuations may remain as strong as ever, if one examines the current patterns and extent of marital assimilation or the reality of 'black ghettoization'.[4] In fact, the largest American Standard Metropolitan Statistical Areas exhibit increasingly elevated segregation index scores over the last thirty years. Increased residential segregation by census tract and census block is now a national phenomenon, a pattern which is not restricted to the large, northern inner-city. Inter-racial marriage remains the exception not the norm and true primary interaction patterns (not those which are time constrained by work, the university, or school setting) remain highly racially enclosed. When enclosure is not present, it is the white male who is the likely sanctioner and most frequent initiator of social change. Such is the reality of U.S. racial social etiquette.[5]

Two further statements in regard to the concepts of racism and prejudice are necessary. Since relative to whites, most blacks lack power (blacks lack the position and thus the ability to get whites to adhere to their, *i.e.* black, will), black prejudice is *not* as significant as white prejudice. Black prejudice seldom gets transmuted into racist behavior. Probably, blacks *are* prejudiced, but they lack the power enjoyed by most whites. Thus blacks are often prejudiced but not racist toward whites! I would also suggest to Wilbanks that he re-examine his utilization of the concept of institutional racism, a term which he utilizes but fails to fully, succinctly or clearly define in his reverse discrimination approach. A modified version of Downs 'institutional subordination' (1976:45) definition as an operational definition of 'institutional racism' would be useful. 'Institutional racism' would refer to "placing or keeping persons in a position or status of inferiority by means of actions or institutional structures which do not use color itself as the subordinating mechanism, but instead use other mechanisms indirectly related to color." The key issue is *result, not intent*. Institutional racism is often the legacy of overt racism, of *de facto* practices that often get codified, and thus sanctioned by *de jure* mechanisms. Examples of institutional racism include: the hiring of white guards and law enforcement officers; the election of white court officials; the implementation of 'objective', Eurocentric testing procedures that select the most Eurocentric non-white available; and the subsequent institutionalization of seniority procedures that penalize the historically excluded — those viewed as having 'contributed less' and as Judge Crockett has noted, have been viewed as 'less than human' [atavistic], 'a threat' to American values, beliefs and practices and 'not [quite] belonging' in white America.

Point Two

According to the DT, Wilbanks concludes "all or most blacks (the pervasiveness factor) are subject to harsher treatment by the system and that the extent of the extra harshness (magnitude factor) is substantial". Such a contention is without statistical support, and merits further examination. Black academics and criminal justice practitioners have not been systematically polled regarding their position on either the pervasiveness or the magnitude factor; however, the *Gallup Report*[6] does substantiate the Wilbanks' claim that the general 'black' populace believes that the U.S. criminal justice 'system' is more punitive toward blacks than toward whites. This same poll also notes that 'non-whites' in general share this belief. Wilbanks contends that this erroneous belief on the part of 'blacks and liberals' is, in part, due to past and currently non-existent, discriminatory practices within the U.S. criminal justice system. However, Wilbanks neglects to mention that such patterns persist in the area of administrative detention as well as in the realm of capital punishment sentencing, among others. For example, this pattern also persists in the area of sentence implementation and sentence commutation, especially when the victim was white.[7] Capital punishment for the crime of rape has traditionally been reserved for blacks and to a lesser extent other non-whites who allegedly raped whites. Death sentences and the denial of their commutation remain a black reality as does the housing of whites in administrative detention and protective custody in jails and prisons across this nation-state. The usual rationalization for such protective custody action is the need to prevent homosexual rape and assault of whites (often white youths) by predatory black offenders as well as to prevent other alleged racially motivated predatory behavior by black inmates. However, do not predatory blacks also aggress against youthful, isolated, passive or effeminate black inmates?

Point Three

Wilbanks is correct in noting that limited information based upon sound research is insufficient to determine whether black decision-makers (police officers, judges, correctional staff) 'make a difference' with respect to the treatment of blacks who are processed by the 'system'. However, one should not be surprised if survey and other research into the practice of black decision-makers on black offenders, showed either no difference or even a negative difference (more severe treatment of black offenders by black decision makers). The criminal justice system is by definition a conservative *status quo* maintenance system. Certainly, in decision-making and line positions, the selection of employees is Eurocentric (Georges-Abeyie, 1984, 1987).

Point Four

Wilbanks rejects the DT thesis because, in part, he claims that many studies have found that blacks receive more lenient treatment than whites at the judicial phase of the criminal justice process. If such is the case, one is likely to find that the DT thesis is supported when one notes the race factor in the victim/assailant relationship (Howard, 1967; Wolfgang and Riedel, 1973, 1975). Black offenders who victimize blacks and other low socio-economic status (SES) non-whites probably do receive less severe sentences than whites who victimize blacks of any SES, unless the white-black victimization case is an extreme case of the 'freak show' variety.[8] If severity of sentences is the measure of a victim's worth, then the DT implies that black victims are viewed as having less worth than white victims.

Point Five

Wilbanks' rejection of the DT thesis — because "if the DT is valid and racial disproportionality indicates racism, why is the black/white incarceration gap lowest in the southern states, where prejudice is allegedly less extensive?" — contains numerous biases and fallacious beliefs. Wilbanks confuses racism for prejudice (*i.e.* attitude for behavior), the very reality he rails against earlier in his text. There is very little evidence that would substantiate the belief that white racism is institutional and less severe in the northeast, southwest, northwest and midwest than in the traditional Old South. One needs to examine the tri-partite issues of general valuations, specific valuations, and the actualization of the specific valuations before speaking about regional differentiation in white prejudice and racism. It is doubtful that white institutional racism (the actualization of the specific valuation) and to a lesser extent, race-specific valuations, differ markedly by region. In fact, Christianson (1984) found that white racism was most severe in several states with relatively few blacks as permanent residents, if racism is associated with black per capita incarceration rates.

Point Six

Regardless of region, when one examines the black/white incarceration gap, one must question within which category Hispanics are to be included. For example, in Florida, criminal justice statistics include Hispanics under the white category, thus, lessening 'the black/white incarceration gap'. Data from other states should be examined for a similar impact upon the black/white incarceration gap. Wilbanks' uses selective scenarios such as the Bernhard Goetz case, Miami crime incidents and so forth to support his argument that blacks systematically select whites to victimize. This reverse 'victimization' argument deserves scrutiny and condemnation. In the Goetz case, the acquittal on attempted homicide and other grand and petit jury findings were probably related to the judge's instructions to the jury (*i.e.* when the alleged charges and crimes were being defined and explained to the lay jury). This instructional procedure would probably be defined by Dr. Wilbanks as an informal factor outside of the realm of empirical study. Yet this procedure, acted out thousands of times daily, does impact upon petit and grand jury findings. As for the Miami crime incidents and other possibly unique crime occurrences, exceptions neither validate nor establish the rule.

Point Seven

Wilbanks' rejects the DT because "if the DT is valid, if blacks are more likely to be punished for attacking whites and if whites are less likely to be punished for attacking blacks, why do black offenders choose white victims more frequently than black victims, and why do white offenders rarely attack blacks?" Such faulty logic merits pages of analysis and response. Wilbanks' inclusion of prison rape, robbery and assault data in order to conclude that the black offender in assault, rape, and robbery chooses white victims more often than s/he chooses black victims is grossly misleading. It also distorts the reality of the rape, assault, and robbery dynamic. The alleged preponderance of black rape, robbery, and assault of white prisoners *is* a possibility, a possibility due, in part, to the spatial proximity of black-white prisoner residence. However, such a proximity is not a common reality in the slum-ghetto environment. It is the residential reality of low status (and increasingly middle and upper status) black Americans. For many years, geographers and social ecologists have examined the criminal's 'journey to work' (Georges-Abeyie and Harries, 1980; Harries, 1974; Harries and Brunn, 1982; Brantingham and Brantingham, 1981). To aggregate prison rape, assault, and robbery statistics (or to utilize that unique universe of statistical data) with rape, assault, and robbery statistics for victim/assailant race factors in the 'free world' setting is to seriously distort the reality of the criminal victimization dynamic in the 'free world' setting. One must also ask about the reality of the race dynamic for the other F.B.I. Part-One offenses such as personal larceny, and household burglary. Criminal victimization data collected by the U.S. Department of Justice includes various reasons for not reporting criminal victimization which differ by race.

In neighborhoods such as the South Bronx, the best predictor for an incident being reported, or not, was likely to have been whether the 'victim' and/or the 'assailant' needed hospitalization or the attention of a mortician. Many of the 'assault' reports were initiated by third parties such as attendant doctors, medics, and social workers. Many of the 'assaults', a criminal term (formal), were not viewed as 'assaults' by the alleged 'victims', especially if the 'assault' did not involve involuntary sex or sex with a pre-adolescent. Clearly, Wilbanks does not understand, or chooses to ignore, the reality of the ethnically or racially enclosed offender-victim dynamic of slum-ghetto existence, a reality that limits communication between slum-ghetto residents and middle class, black and white, usually Eurocentric, police officials who neither live in the neighborhood, nor share the subcultural or contracultural values of the neighborhood residents.

CONCLUSION

Wilbanks' challenge to the traditional conflict and labeling approaches is thorough and extremely well organized. His bibliography is excellent. He raises numerous research questions and offers findings that deserve attention. However, his bias, a consensus and reverse labeling approach that denies the DT whenever the DT cannot allegedly be 'proven', is an approach that deserves serious examination. Limiting his study to the formal decision making process; conceptualizing the black community as homogeneous along ethnic, SES, and spatial lines; selectively using anecdotal and 'research findings'; and uncritically accepting the extent of inter-racial criminality involving black assailants and white victims all deserve condemnation. Most importantly, any approach that would mask its criminological and social biases behind the façade of research parameters and questions needs to be seriously examined and challenged.

The Myth of a Racist Criminal Justice System is an important book because it implies the existence of value-free criminological and criminal justice research methodology based upon empiricism. It also highlights the need for a criminological and criminal justice theory which is grounded in the experiential reality of non-whites from a slum-ghetto, non-Eurocentric background. Such a perspective might lend qualified support to the DT. Not in the manner which Wilbanks dictates — *not* by stating that the U.S. criminal justice 'process' is a system that always or usually discriminates in a systematic manner. Rather, it might frame the hypothesis differently as a rather disjointed series of processes that may discriminate periodically against certain blacks of specific ethnicity, or SES, and spatial domain. This grounded theory may note that relatively affluent and urban blacks of specific ethnic backgrounds who victimize blacks, or whites, of specific SES and or race and ethnicity, are punished more severely than their white or other black counterparts. Such a grounded theory might note that the focus of race-related research should be cognizant of the effect of site and situational factors in the victimization dynamic, as well as such factors as SES, age, and 'black' ethnicity, not just race, when the victim-assailant relationship is noted. Such a grounded theory might note the possibility of a heretofore undocumented 'black power' component (Curtis, 1975) in the criminal victimization of whites — a component that escalates an intended burglary into an aggravated assault, robbery, rape, or homicide. Such a grounded theoretical approach might also note the significance of 'Petit Apartheid' victimizations (i.e., indignities) that go unreported, and thus undocumented, yet nonetheless indelibly impact upon community/police relations, and expectations.

ENDNOTES

1. See the most recent Uniform Crime Report; U.S. Department of Justice,1987/88; Florida Department of Justice,1988.

2. See, for example, Georges-Abeyie, 1984; McNeely and Pope, 1981; Wright,1987; and Flowers,1988.

3. For example, note the 'salient factor score' utilized by the federal parole commission as well as Joan Petersilia's work (1983, 1984, 1985, 1988) or the relatively new restrictions on the police use of deadly force.

4. For a discussion see 1980 and post 1980 Bureau of the Census reports.

5. That is the upper status reference group sanctions the out-group referencing as evidenced by the white male-black female dating and marriage patterns of the later 1980s.

6. *The Gallup Report*, January 11-14/85 examines the application of the death penalty.

7. Note the April, 1987 U.S. Supreme Court *McClesky* v. *Georgia* ruling which, on a 5 to 4 vote, rejected the racial bias challenge to the death penalty, a challenge that utilized statistical data collected by Dr. David Baldus, a University of Iowa Law Professor. Much of the data was based upon Baldus *et al* ,1983; Schaeffer, 1984; Tauber and Tauber, 1965; U.S. Dept. of Justice, 1987.

8. One example of such is the Philadelphia Gary Heidnik case which involved the rape, murder, and torture of black women as well as possible cannibalism by a white assailant.

REFERENCES

American Enterprise Institute, *Public Opinion*. Washington, D.C.

Baldus, D. C., C. Pulaski, and G. Woodworth (1983) "Comparative Review of Death Sentences: An Empirical Study of the Georgia Experience" *Journal of Criminal Law and Criminology*, 74:661-725

Block, R. *Violent Crime*, Lexington, MA: D.C. Heath.

Brantingham, P. J. and P. L. Brantingham (eds.), (1981), *Environmental Criminology*, Beverly Hills: Sage Publications.

Christianson, S. (1984) "Out Black Prisons" *The Criminal Justice System and Blacks*, New York: Clark Boardman, Ltd:307-314.

Curtis, L. A. (1975) *Violence, Race, and Culture*, Lexington, MA: D.C. Heath.

Downs, A. (1976) *Urban Problems and Prospects* (2nd. Ed.). Chicago: Rand McNally College Publishing Company.

Florida, Department of Law Enforcement (1988) *Crime in Florida: 1988 Annual Report*, Tallahassee, FL: Florida Department of Law Enforcement.

Gallup Organization Inc. *Gallup Report*. Princeton, N. J. Published Monthly.

Gallup Organization Inc.*Gallup Report* Interview Date 1/11-14/85; Survey #245-G.

Georges-Abeyie, D. E. (Ed.) (1984) *The Criminal Justice System and Blacks*, New York: Clark Boardman, Ltd.

Georges-Abeyie, D. E. and K. Harries (Eds.) (1980) *Crime: A Spatial Perspective*, New York: Columbia University Press.

Georges-Abeyie, D. E. (1989) "Race, Ethnicity, and the Spatial Dynamic: Toward a Realistic Study of Black Crime, Crime Victimization, and Criminal Justice Processing of Blacks" *Social Justice*, 16 (4):35-54.

Georges-Abeyie, D. E. (1981) "Studying Black Crime: A Realistic Approach" in P. J. Brantingham and P. L. Brantingham (eds) *Environmental Criminology*. Beverly Hills: Sage Publications.

Georges-Abeyie, D. E. (1974) "The Issues is Racism Not Busing: It's Caste Not Class — An Exploration of the Application of Cognitive Dissonance Theory". A Paper Presented to the Association of American Geographers.

Harries, K. D. and S. D. Brunn (1982) *The Geography of Urban Crime*, New York: Longman, Inc.

Harries, K.D.(1974) *The Geography of Crime and Justice*, New York: McGraw Hill.

Howard Sr., J. (1967) *Administration of Race Cases in the City of Baltimore and the State of Maryland*, Baltimore: Monumental Bar Association

Lieberson, S. (1963) *Ethnic Patterns in American Cities*, New York: Free Press

McClesky v. *Georgia* Ruling 22 April 1987.

McNeely, R. L. and Carl E. Pope (eds) (1981) *Race, Crime and Criminal Justice*, Beverly Hills, CA: Sage.

Parrillo, V. N. (1985) *Strangers to These Shores* (2nd. Ed) New York: Wiley.

Petersilia, J. (1983) *Racial Disparities in The Criminal Justice System*, Santa Monica, CA: Rand Corporation.

Schaeffer, R. T. (1984) *Racial and Ethnic Groups* (2nd. Ed.) Boston: Little, Brown

Taeuber, Karl E. and Alma F. Taeuber. Negroes in Cities. Chicago: Aldine Publishing Company, 1965

U.S., Department of Justice (1987) *Correctional Populations in the United States*, Washington, D.C.

U.S., Department of Justice (1988) *Report to the Nation on Crime and Justice*, Washington, D.C.: Bureau of Justice Statistics.

Westie, F. R. (1965) "The American Dilemma: An Empirical Test" *American Sociological Review*, 30:531-532.

Wolfgang, M. and M. Riedel (1973) "Race and the Death Penalty in Georgia." *American Journal of Orthopsychiatry*, 45 (4):658-688.

Wolfgang, M. and M. Riedel (1973) "Race, Judicial Discretion and the Death Penalty" *Annals of the American Academy of Political and Social Science*, 407:119-133.

Wright, B. (1987) *Black Robes, White Justice*, Secaucus, NJ: Lyle Stuart Inc.

CHAPTER 7

Racial Bias and Criminal Justice:
Definitional and Methodological Issues

Michael J. Lynch
Florida State University

I have been asked to comment on Wilbanks' *The Myth of a Racist Criminal Justice System.* This book is difficult to attack because it is carefully conceived and generates an emotional response from its critics. This is exactly the type of response Wilbanks is most capable or repelling.

Wilbanks' attack upon discrimination theory (DT) is disarming because it begins by recognizing the validity of both the DT and the no-discrimination perspective (NDT), and asserts that the literature on racial discrimination proves neither the DT or NDT theses. Further, he notes that proof for either position is gathered through a process of selectively attending to evidence supporting or denying racism. I do not disagree with this assessment of the *literature*, and if Wilbanks' critique had focused solely upon this issue, it would be acceptable. However, from this beginning, he argues selectively (the same thing he accuses DT theorists of doing) and proceeds as if the literature proves the NDT (throughout arguing in an apologetic way against the literature demonstrating DT). His approach is hardly as unbiased as his introductory remarks make it appear.

Another way Wilbanks disarms his critics is by conceding the history of racism that characterized American development. He reinterprets racial discrimination and claims, like Reiman, that it has evolved into class discrimination. Again, I do not disagree. He makes the mistake, unlike Reiman, of dismissing the connection between class and race as spurious or "incidental" (p. 60). Much sociological literature suggests that this relationship is not incidental, but reflects a long history of racial discrimination. As a result, racial discrimination in modern American society operates through class, with its effect resting most fully upon minority groups. By maintaining a bias against specific social classes (as Wilbanks demonstrates throughout his book), the criminal justice system does indeed contribute to racial discrimination. In this way, racial discrimination is masked or mystified by class discrimination.

Reprinted with permission from *The Critical Criminologist* Vol. 2, No. 1, Spring, 1990

Wilbanks defines racism as a conscious atempt to discriminate against a particular race. Such a definition of racism is difficult to prove or falsify. Had he instead focused on racial bias, or on outcomes without reference to intent, his conclusions might have been different. Thus, the definitional basis of Wilbanks' NDT argument is virtually impossible to dispute empirically, if one operates according to this strict definition of racism.

I do not believe, however, that we must consciously design racial discrimination into the system before we can say it is racist. In the first place, systems do not have consciousness; they operate according to organizational criteria. In the second place, the history of racism in the U.S. established selection criteria (e.g., in arrests, bail, etc.) that were clearly discriminatory (they favored whites, and the middle class). Since we have failed to alter these selection criteria, the system continues to operate in a racist manner, even if we no longer hold such values; even if we are unaware this is occurring. Thus, unless we make or have at some point made a conscious attempt to alter these criteria, the history of conscious racial practices seeps into punishment decisions.

In his discussion of punishment in *The Division of Labor*, Durkheim noted: "The nature of practice does not necessarily change because the conscious intentions of those who apply it are modified. It might, in truth, still play the same role as before without being perceived" (p. 87). In short, even if we are conscious of racial bias and do not intend to participate in this bias, it may still become manifest in the punishment process because it is built in. Similarly, Wilbanks' assertion that racism is a conscious process overlooks a vast psychological literature that painstakingly examines how individuals repress thought processes that create psychological dissonance. Thus, racism can be an unconscious process, and most likely has been tucked away in the American unconscious.

One of the major problems in Wilbanks' book is his omission of a definition or discussion of race. For example, race could have been examined as a social construction. In this view, race definitions reflect power relationships within society, not necessarily visual cues like skin color (although these cues are the easiest way to identify such groups). Those without power are generally defined as belonging to minority groups. Szymanski suggests that a group is defined as a race when its economic role becomes differentiated and inheritable over generations. In this sociological context, race *cannot* be understood apart from class, something Wilbanks fails to recognize. This understanding of race calls Wilbanks' rejection of the connection between race and class into question.

Wilbanks also fails to address the haphazard way in which race is determined by various parts of the criminal justice system, or variations in race measures across states and jurisdictions (ranging from appearance to sir-name identification). This leads to other problems as well. For example, how are light skinned blacks with 'white-cultural' names classified? Such problems affect any statistical analysis of racial discrimination. Available data may not, in other words, reflect the true extent of racism.

Further, much research into racial discrimination employs a black/white dichotomy. The problem with black/white or black/not-black race measures is that non-black minority groups get lumped together with white-majority groups. This practice confounds attempts to assess racial bias by suppressing race dependent outcome variations, and makes a NDT finding more likely. Neither Wilbanks' literature review or analysis is sensitive to this issue, and much of the literature he sites shows NDT precisely because it uses a black/white instead of white/not white (equivalent to a white/minority race dichotomy) operationalization of the race variable.

White/non-white research recognizes the possibility that all racial minority groups, not just blacks, suffer from discrimination. Wilbanks recognizes the possibility that other groups suffer from race discrimination, but limits this assertion to whites (the majority). His argument that racial discrimination could operate against whites is important and should not be overlooked or dismissed completely (this might happen in certain jurisdictions). The question, according to Wilbanks' own criteria for determining race discrimination, is whether this is (1) a conscious practice that is (2) systematically engineered. While he shows that there is at times an apparent anti-white sentiment, he provides no evidence that this bias is *systematic*. (In short, while arguing for white discrimination, he forgets his own definition of racism). And, indeed, if we accept his proposition that the bias against whites is systematic, then we must also accept the stronger association he demonstrates against blacks.

The white discrimination argument is also misleading since white discrimination does not necessarily cancel the effect of black discrimination. Aggregate data (the type Wilbanks employs in his Appendix) contains the influences of both processes. Thus, if aggregate data demonstrates DT (measured as percent increases in ratio of blacks to whites from arrest to incarceration, as Wilbanks does) this finding cannot be dismissed on the grounds that there is reverse discrimination occurring simultaneously against whites. This is so because aggregate data reflect the effects of both tendencies. Thus, the bias against whites has been controlled for by employing aggregate data. If a bias still emerges against blacks, then we know

37

that its magnitude (a measure Wilbanks endorses) is greater than the bias against whites, and that the systematic nature of this bias is evident despite any other forms of bias.

In addition, Wilbanks' implicit definition of the criminal justice system is narrow and focuses upon processing outcomes. But, such outcomes cannot be discussed outside of the relationships of this system to law, since the criminal justice system is designed to uphold law. In short, Wilbanks fails to analyze the racial biases contained within law. These biases are important since they effect decisions to arrest, an aspect of the criminal justice process that Wilbanks does not sufficiently analyze. If, for example, we can support Wilbanks' claim that there is no systematic racism because blacks are no more likely than whites to be punished in a particular manner, we cannot reject the possibility that blacks are selectively processed at the unmeasured stage: arrest. Thus, the courts may not be biased, but the arrest mechanism could be. Whether this amounts to a systematic race bias is open for debate since one part of the system demonstrates race bias while another part does not.

Having read Wilbanks' book, I am confused as to how one determines what level of statistical association demonstrates racial discrimination, especially since he rejects statistical significance as an important criteria. Statistical significance cannot be rejected out of hand, as Wilbanks does, because this measure tells us that the difference between race and outcome *is not* occurring by *chance*. This is true regardless of sample size. In rejecting tests of statistical significance, Wilbanks argues in favor of examining the magnitude of the relationship. Such a measure, however, is misleading in that we could find very large differences that are not statistically significant (they occur by chance and are not systematic). Both measures should be considered, but tests of significance remain important, despite Wilbanks' assertion. They allow us to separate patterned from random variation. And if NDT suggests that race bias is systematic, it must demonstrate that race related findings are indeed random, not systematic or patterned.

In this light let us consider Wilbanks' discussion of race and processing outcomes: "the racial gap in California for 1980 increased *by only* 19 percent from arrest to imprisonment...." (p. 145; my emphasis). This statement is mystified by the qualifying words "by only". These data imply that blacks are, to the tune of 19 times in 100, more likely to receive different treatment than white defendants. An acceptable chance variation would be 1 in 100 or even 5 in 100 cases, not 19 in 100. And, this comparison omits from consideration the racial bias exerted against other minority groups (e.g. Hispanics) which would inflate the differences noted here.

Given Wilbanks' qualification of the 19 percent increase in black/white ratios from arrest to incarceration as "only 19 percent", I would like to know what magnitude of change in black/white ratios constitutes discrimination. Is, for example, the 68 percent increase in the ratio of black males age 20-29 to white males ages 20-29 from arrest to incarceration sufficient? (see Table 3 of Wilbanks' book appended here). Or is this still an insufficient criteria? And, at what level of aggregation does this effect have to be demonstrated? The local level? The state level? The national level? With these issues in mind, let us take a closer look at Table 5 presented in the Appendix to Wilbanks' book (appended here).

These data examine black/white ratios at 6 decision points (from arrest to incarceration) in California for 19 offenses. This Table indicates that for 12 of 19 offenses, or for 63 % of reported offense types (selection criteria for offenses is not discussed), the ratio of blacks to whites across these 6 points increased between 4 to 93 percent (statistically insignificant or non-systematic in 2 cases: abduction and public order). For the remaining 7 offenses, the ratio decreased from 4 to 40 percent, indicating discrimination against whites (statistically insignificant or non-systematic in 2 cases: dangerous drugs and fondling children). Using Wilbanks' measure, the average magnitude of the effect against blacks for these 12 offenses was 30.9 percent, while the average magnitude of the effect against whites was 12.4 percent. If we separate these effects by the seriousness of offense[1] we find: (1) average magnitude of the effect against blacks for serious crime is 24.6 percent; against whites, 12 percent; (2) average magnitude of the effect against blacks for less serious offenses is 43.5 percent; against whites, 8 percent; and (3) blacks are disadvantaged in 8 of 10 serious crimes, while whites are disadvantaged on 5 of 9 lesser offenses. From this data we could conclude two things. First, considering *magnitude of effects*, as Wilbanks suggests, we would conclude that blacks were at a greater disadvantage for both serious and lesser crimes. Second, if we consider proportions of offenses for which each group was disadvantaged we would conclude that blacks are disadvantaged for serious crime (8 times in 10) while whites are disadvantaged for lesser crimes (5 times in 9). One could argue from such data that there either is or is not evidence of systematic race bias, depending, of course, on how one chooses to define systematic bias. (In Pennsylvania a similar picture emerges, see Table 6 of Wilbanks' book. Blacks are disadvantaged, in terms of magnitude, for serious crimes, while whites are disadvantaged for lesser offenses. Thus, even across jurisdictions, there is evidence that blacks are disadvantaged for serious offenses. This picture is obscured by the manner in which Wilbanks aggregates these data).

Finally, Wilbanks' selective focus on Pennsylvania and California is also misleading, but plays directly into his theory of reverse discrimination. These data (Appendix Tables 5 and 6 of Wilbanks' book) demonstrate discrimination against blacks in California, but against whites in Pennsylvania. These two effects do not cancel, however, as Wilbanks asserts, given the magnitude of the relationship in California. One could conclude, as Wilbanks does, from this evidence that there is no systematic race bias, but only if we interpret each state's criminal justice system as comprising a part of a 'united criminal justice system'. Leading researchers in this area, like David Duffee, argue against this 'system view' of criminal justice processes employed by Wilbanks.

In conclusion, Wilbanks' support for the NDT is highly dependent upon: how discrimination/racism is defined; how one measures race; how one interprets criminal justice data (significance or magnitude); how we determine the threshold for discrimination; level of aggregation; the meaning of the term 'systematic bias'; and the type of crimes examined. Having read Wilbanks' work and examined his data, I am not inclined to agree with his conclusions that a systematic race bias is in no way evident in the criminal justice system.

ENDNOTES

1. For purposes of this discussion, serious offenses are those designated in Part I of The Uniform Crime Report (UCR), and lesser offenses are those designated in Part II of the UCR. With reference to Wilbanks' Table 5, the first ten offenses listed are considered *serious* crimes and the remaining nine offenses as lesser offenses. In Table 6, the first eight offenses plus 'auto theft', 'weapon offense' and 'on person' were considered serious crimes.

APPENDIX I: THREE TABLES FROM WILBANKS

Table 3: Gaps by race, sex, and selected age groups at 5 decision points of the California CJS in 1980[1]

	Arrest	Sent to pros.[a]	Not dropped[b]	Conv.[c]	Conv. as fel.[d]	Incar. prison[e]	%change arrest to prison[f]
Black/white	5.21:1	4.79:1	4.40:1	4.17:1	4.86:1	6.18:1	+ 19%
Male/female	7.01:1	6.90:1	6.86:1	7.10:1	7.56:1	18.59:1	+164%
Black male/white male	5.05:1	4.79:1	4.40:1	4.13:1	4.78:1	6.19:1	+ 23%
Black female/white female	5.13:1	4.98:1	4.59:1	4.64:1	5.65:1	6.99:1	+ 36%
Black male 20-29/white male 20-29	3.88:1	3.67:1	3.38:1	3.21:1	3.74:1	6.52:1	+ 68%
Black female 20-29/white female 20-29	4.10:1	3.97:1	3.67:1	3.73:1	4.42:1	6.02:1	+ 47%

1. Source: Adapted from Wilbanks (1987); a. Indicates those forwarded by the police to the prosecutor before a court disposition; c. Indicates cases where a conviction resulted.; d. Indicates that the conviction (or at least one if multiple convictions) was for a felony.; e. Indicates that a prison sentence was given.; f. Indicates the percentage increase in the gap from arrest to incarceration in prison.

Table 5: Black/white gaps at 6 decision points of the California CJS for 19 offenses in 1980

Offense	Arrest	Sent to pros.[a]	Not dropped[b]	Conv.[c]	Conv. as fel.[d]	Incar. prison[e]	%change arrest to prison[f]
Neg. mansl — vehicle	1.41:1	1.40:1	1.43:1	1.53:1	1.69:1	1.72:1	+22%
Homicide	6.47:1	6.32:1	6.09:1	5.76:1	5.83:1	5.69:1	-12%
Abduction	5.68:1	5.19:1	6.54:1	4.56:1	5.22:1	5.96:1	+ 4%
Rape	7.27:1	7.22:1	6.12:1	5.82:1	6.39:1	9.12:1	+ 25%
Robbery	9.42:1	8.95:1	8.56:1	8.18:1	8.49:1	8.32:1	-12%
Aggr. assault — weapon	5.14:1	4.88:1	4.52:1	4.05:1	5.27:1	7.70:1	+50%
Assault	3.59:1	3.50:1	3.16:1	2.74:1	3.52:1	5.47:1	+52%
Burglary	4.34:1	4.16:1	4.03:1	3.81:1	4.03:1	5.39:1	+24%
Larceny	5.51:1	5.32:1	4.99:1	4.75:1	5.10:1	6.35:1	+15%
Motor vehicle theft	5.84:1	5.40:1	5.16:1	5.02:1	5.48:1	6.16:1	+ 5%
Forgery	6.06:1	5.83:1	5.68:1	5.62:1	5.62:1	5.47:1	-10%
Fraud	5.53:1	5.36:1	5.22:1	5.28:1	5.59:1	6.67:1	+21%
Selling marijuana	6.00:1	5.76:1	5.10:1	4.60:1	3.46:1	5.70:1	- 5%
Possessing marijuana	3.33:1	3.19:1	2.55:1	2.85:1	2.78:1	5.18:1	+56%
Dangerous drugs	5.68:1	5.52:1	4.77:1	4.62:1	6.11:1	5.47:1	- 4%
Fondling children	2.02:1	1.99:1	1.71:1	1.49:1	1.69:1	1.93:1	- 4%
Weapon offense	2.35:1	2.25:1	2.10:1	1.94:1	2.13:1	4.53:1	+93%
Driving while intoxicated	1.21:1	1.21:1	1.19:1	1.20:1	1.22:1	0.73:1	-40%
Public order	4.05:1	3.96:1	3.18:1	3.12:1	3.55:1	4.23:1	+ 4%
All offenses	5.21:1	4.79:1	4.40:1	4.17:1	4.86:1	6.18:1	+19%

1. Source: Adapted from Wilbanks (1987); a Indicates those arrested by the police and forwarded to the prosecutor; b Indicates that the cases at this point were not dropped by the prosecutor before a court disposition; c Indicates conviction in court; d Indicates conviction as a felony rather than as a misdemeanor; e Indicates a prison sentence; f Indicates the percentage of change in the black/white gap from arrest to prison g Numbers in parentheses are National Crime Information Center offense codes.

Table 6: Black/white gaps for 16 offense categories at 5 decision points of the Pennsylvania CJS in 1980[1]

	Arrest & sent to pros.[a]	Not dropped[b]	Conv.[c]	Conv. as felon[d]	Incar. prison[e]	5 or more. years[f]	%change arrest to incar.[g]
Negligent manslaughter	1.0:1	1.0:1	0.8:1	1.0:1	1.9:1	h	+ 9%
Homicide	14.1:1	1.2:1	18.9:1	16.6:1	30.8:1	34.8:1	+118%
Rape	21.8:1	21.7:1	22.0:1	23.9:1	26.8:1	47.5:1	+ 23%
Sexual assault	2.5:1	2.5:1	2.8:1	2.5:1	5.5:1	12.2:1	+120%
Robbery	30.5:1	29.4:1	31.6:1	30.5:1	18.0:1	26.5:1	-41%
Simple assault	6.4:1	6.1:1	7.6:1	6.6:1	8.9:1	25.1:1	+ 39%
Assault	11.0:1	10.6:1	12.6:1	11.4:1	16.3:1	27.3:1	+ 48%
Burglary	2.4:1	2.4:1	1.8:1	2.4:1	1.4:1	2.0:1	-42%
Shoplifting	29.7:1	29.1:1	40.0:1	30.3:1	8.5:1	h	-71%
Auto theft	10.7:1	10.0:1	8.4:1	10.4:1	3.0:1	4.9:1	-72%
Fraud	4.6:1	4.5:1	4.7:1	4.5:1	2.4:1	4.5:1	-48%
Stolen property	7.5:1	7.6:1	7.4:1	7.7:1	3.7:1	8.8:1	-51%
Resisting arrest	5.1:1	4.9:1	4.1:1	6.3:1	1.9:1	h	-63%
Weapon offense	18.1:1	18.6:1	20.7:1	20.6:1	12.5:1	14.2:1	-31%
On person	5.1:1	4.7:1	4.5:1	4.8:1	7.3:1	5.7:1	+ 43%
Public order	4.7:1	4.3:1	4.4:1	3.9:1	6.7:1	15.7:1	+ 43%
All 16 above	8.3:1	6.7:1	9.0:1	8.6:1	7.9:1	15.7:1	- 5%
All offenses	8.1:1	7.9:1	8.7:1	8.4:1	7.4:1	15.5:1	- 9%

1. Source: Adapted from Wilbanks, 1987; a. Indicates those arrested by the police and forwarded to the prosecutor; (In Pennsylvania no cases were released by the police, as was the case in California.); b. Indicates cases at this point were not dropped by the prosecutor before a court disposition; c. Indicates cases where a conviction resulted; d. Indicates that the conviction (or at least one if multiple convictions) was for a felony; e. Indicates that a prison sentence was given; f. Indicates prison term of 5 or more years; g. Indicates the percentage increase or decrease in the gap or rate ratio from arrest to incarceration in prison; h. Cannot calculate, since one or fewer cases for either or both races.

CHAPTER 8

The Muddled Methodology of The Wilbanks NDT Thesis

Zaid Ansari
University of Cincinnati

INTRODUCTION

This paper addresses several serious methodological problems with William Wilbanks' *The Myth of a Racist Criminal Justice System* (1987).

Wilbanks' fundamental methodological difficulty stems from his premise that "systematic racial discrimination against blacks in the American Criminal Justice system is difficult to prove." This issue has been addressed in a related paper by Lynch (1990).

Instead of discussing Wilbanks' operational definitions of how critical decisions "favor" blacks over whites or his definition of racism in the criminal justice system, and other anecdotal comments used to support this empirical discussion (Wilbanks, 1987: 157), this paper will address his analysis of the Offender Based Transaction Statistics (OBTS) data used to test his NDT thesis.

The following topics relating to Wilbanks' methodology will be critiqued and suggestions will be made and alternatives for his methodology will be presented in the following order: (1) the use of bivariate contingency table analysis; (2) the inappropriate use of proportional reduction error measures; (3) the absence of interaction terms and "test factors" to control for confounding effects; (4) collapsing discrete categories across levels of the OBTS data decision points; (5) the inherent sample selection biases; (6) logistic regression, and log linear analysis as alternatives to bivariate contingency analysis; and (7) decision and conclusion.

BIVARIATE CONTINGENCY ANALYSIS

Wilbanks' use of a bivariate contingency table analysis with race as the only predictor for a dichotomous outcome across eight to ten decision levels in the criminal justice system, using the Offender Based Transaction Statistics for 1980, does not answer the salient issues raised by his NDT thesis.

Reprinted with permission from *The Critical Criminologist* Vol. 2, No. 1, Spring, 1990

Rosenberg (1968), Hirschi (1969) and Davis (1971) have demonstrated that bivariate associations and their accompanying test statistics and measures of association should be viewed with extreme caution. Moreover, these bivariate associations can only demonstrate some very preliminary etiological assumptions in the absence of a properly specified and controlled model (Davis, 1971: 112).

The introduction of relevant controls, as noted by Rosenberg (1968), elaborates and refines the bivariate relationship. Wilbanks' conclusion of no, or only residual, discrimination without introducing theoretically relevant test factors at each decision point leaves several of the rival threats either of a spurious, anteceding, intervening, and, more importantly, a suppressing nature, suspect. Wilbanks' lack of the use of controls and his not constructing interaction terms, that are readily available in the OBTS data, raises serious doubts concerning how thorough his review of the literature was with reference to racial bias and the criminal justice system.

Rosenberg illustrates the effect of a suppresser variable by discussing Middletons' classic analysis of alienation and cultural estrangement (1968: 85-86). In this study, which was built on an earlier analysis by Seeman, little differences were found between blacks and whites on an alienation scale using a bivariate analysis. However, when Middleton introduced education as a control and blacks and white were compared, whites were found to be more alienated than blacks. The original relationship was thus concealed by the suppression of education at each level. Rosenberg further asserts that the reason of no difference in the bivariate relationship was due to the fact that poorly educated people are more culturally estranged and blacks are more poorly educated (1968: 87).

There are several suspect suppresser variables that may exist in many bivariate relationships of ascribed attributes. This is particularly true given the fact social differences are often predicted by the ascribed attributes (Trigg, 1987: 72-76). Apparently, Wilbanks' NDT thesis was not concerned with controlling for the general offense levels using, for example, variable 47, or for the pre-trial status (variable 49, Inter-Consortium for Political and Social Research, abbreviated ICPSR, 1980). These variables may have suppressed some of the variation at the early decision levels in the OBTS data. I will address this problem in a forthcoming related paper.

MEASURE OF ASSOCIATION

Wilbanks' use of the uncertainty coefficient as a pre-measure of association across the decision levels of the criminal justice system is inappropriate because of the assumptions of the NDT thesis concerning the structure of the decision outcomes. By adding the additional categories in the Pennsylvania OBTS data (Wilbanks, 1987: 163) the gaps presented as percentages were calculated from marginal distributions that are skewed across the selected race, sex and age groups. Reynolds notes that skewed marginal distributions drastically alter the percentage differences, unless smoothing or standardization is conducted, and attenuates the sensitivity of measures of association (1977: 46). This problem will be discussed later in this paper. Wilbanks' discussion concerning bivariate and multivariate models of unexplained variation, after controls, as being not indicative of a 'race' effect (1987: 196) does not explain away the predictive importance of race, or other relevant variables. Achen (1986) as well as Kennedy (1985) note how one may ascertain the importance of a variables' contribution in a model.

With measurement difficulties well known in social science data, Wilbanks' review of previous studies and his discussion concerning both explained and unexplained variation should be considered as inconclusive with the absence of use of an "errors in variables" model used with instruments to reduce measurement error and thus directly impact the amount of explained variation (Kennedy, 1985: 133).

Greenwood and Zimring (1985: 18) cite Shannon's analysis of West and Farrington's Cambridge longitudinal study to illustrate how the prediction of a juvenile delinquent becoming an adult offender suffers when the measure of association is the unadjusted uncertainty coefficient.

The uncertainty coefficient's logic as a PRE-measure is designed to reduce the number of prediction errors made in predicting the dependent variable when the independent variable is known. The modal category of the marginal distribution for the row or column of the dependent variable is compared to the category of the value predicted by the independent variable and this allows one to find the percentage of errors reduced by dividing the Error by Rule (1) (the error made by predicting an event by the observed categories). The equation stated below illustrates this logic:

$$PRE = \frac{Error\ by\ Rule\ (1) - Error\ by\ Rule\ (2)}{Error\ by\ Rule\ (1)}$$

Instead of relying on this type of PRE-measure alone, Wilbanks should have used the *Relative Improvement Over Change* (RICO) (Greenwood and Zimring, 1985: 19).

The RICO computation in a *2x2* table involves calculating the random correct percentage prediction (RC) that would occur if there was independence. This method involves multiplying the diagonal marginal

45

(row x column) + (row x column). The next step in this process involves finding the percentage of correct predictions for the one tailed hypothesis test.

Thus, to arrive at the improvement over change (IOC) it is necessary to find the difference in the percentage predicted correctly (PC) minus (RC), the random correct percentage, or *PC-RC= IOC*. Next, what Greenwood and Zimring (1985: 19) point out is the necessity of computing the maximum percentage that could have been predicted correctly (MC).

This method is an improvement over the uncertainty coefficient used by Wilbanks in as much as it does not assume that all errors in prediction, whether false positive or false negatives, have equal weight. For instance, police profiles of black youth as drug traffickers are likely to produce false positive predictions of these youths' involvement in drug distribution. The resulting initial arrest percentages would be higher for blacks relative to whites. Thus the RICO method takes into account the structure of the decision problem (Greenwood and Zimring, 1985: 19-21).

Wilbanks argues that those who maintain that there is no 'systematic' discrimination (in the sense that in general blacks are not treated worse than whites 'other things being equal') are correct (1987: 51). Furthermore, Wilbanks argues that racial discrimination against blacks often occurs, but also racial discrimination occurs which favors blacks.

Wilbanks attempts to empirically test the first claim by comparing the percentage difference of "arrest to incarceration" of blacks and whites (1987: 149). He argues that this canceling out effect is evidenced by the +19% increase of Black/White (favoring whites) in the California OBTS data, while the Pennsylvania OBTS data showed a 9% favoring blacks (1987: 163). This observation is a major problem in the interpretation of the canceling effect using Wilbanks' percentages (1987: 163) of unequal categories and collapsed discrete categories of the Pennsylvania OBTS data compared to those of California. He attempts to explain this in a footnote. His assertion is that "In Pennsylvania no cases were released by the police as was in the case of California" (1987: 163). If this was the case for the 1980 OBTS data, two approaches could have been taken by Wilbanks to overcome this problem. First, the additional categories — the odd ratio of "two or more charges" and "two or more convictions" — were present for Pennsylvania and not California. This should have been avoided. These two categories amount to Pennsylvania having a larger number of categories by which to divide variation. Secondly, the California arrest category should have been omitted to insure comparability.

SAMPLE SELECTION BIAS PROBLEMS

The problem associated with the non random selection of sub samples has recently received much deserved attention in criminal justice and criminological research (Berk, 1983; Achen, 1986; Hagan, 1987). Wilbanks' failure to recognize the sample selection process in the 1980 OBTS data presents serious problems of interpretation and makes generalizing virtually impossible.

Berk (1983) points out that when selection bias occurs because of the exclusion of a non-random sub sample of cases due to the presence of either high or low values on some exogenous variable, the result is, as in the case of multiple regression analysis, biased coefficients, and the violation of the linearity assumption, as well as other problems (*ibid.*: 387-389). Thus, Berk demonstrates that for all of the observations with low values of Xi equal to X, the expected value of each y, (estimated y) is biased upward. The opposite is true for the high values of Xi equal to X (Ibid.).

Therefore, in the case of Wilbanks' data, cases dismissed for one reason or another, cases plead down, and selected out because of some non-random mechanism, actually should be viewed as a two part process. The first aspect is a selection equation and the mechanism of selection, although unobserved, is correlated with the criterion of the outcome. The second aspect is the outcome process and it contains the unobserved endogenous variable from the selection process. These two equations must be modeled separately in order to purge the correlated errors across the two equations, eliminate the non-linear function, and correctly specify the process. This topic has been well covered in the court processing literature by Klepper, Nagin, and Tierney (1981) and recently by Talacarico and Myers (1987). By constructing a hazard rate, suggested by Berk (1983: 391), Wilbanks could have then used logistic regression analysis, or log linear contingency table analysis.

Thus, it can be reasonably argued that one cannot determine from Wilbanks' analysis, or even infer from previous studies, that only an unsystematic race effect of a disparate nature occurs in the criminal justice system unless carefully controlled models are corrected for truncation, specification, and measurement errors.

Wilbanks' NDT thesis, when considered in light of its substantive importance to the criminal justice community, could have informed its audience of a significant change in the history of the broader social context of race, class and justice in the United States. His NDT thesis, because of both conceptual difficulties in defining racism and the criminal justice systems favoring of blacks versus whites and whites versus blacks, as well as the accompanying methodological problems, leaves no alternative except to urge further analysis of the NDT thesis.

In conclusion, we must ask ourselves, does the presence of racism in any form within the processes of doing justice cancel its burdening effect to its victims. The impact of racial bias experienced by those in criminal justice system processing cannot be cancelled out by other non-bias events in other states. The effect of racial discrimination is always injurious and can be life altering.

REFERECNCES

Achen, C.(1986) *The Statistical Analysis of Quasi Experiments.* Berkeley: University of California Press.

Berk, R. (1983) "An Introduction to Sample Selection Bias in Sociological Data" *American Sociological Review* 49:386-98.

Davis, J. (1971) *Elementary Survey Analysis.* Englewood Cliffs: Prentice Hall.

Greenwood, P., and F. Zimring (1985) *One More Chance*, Santa Monica: Rand Corporation.

Hagan, John (1987) "Review Essay: A Great Truth in the Study of Crime" *Criminology* 25(2): 421-27.

Hirschi, T. and S. Hanan (1973) *Principles of Survey Analysis.* New York: Free Press.

Kennedy, P. (1985) *A Guide to Econometrics* Oxford: MIT Press.

Klepper, S., D. Nagin and L. Tierney (1981) "Discrimination in the Criminal Justice System: A Critical Appraisal of the Literature and Suggestions for Future Research" Social Science Department, Carnegie Mellon University.

Lynch, M. (1990) "Racial Bias and Criminal Justice: Definitional and Methodological Issues"*The Critical Criminologist* 2(1).

Meyers, M. and S. Talerilo (1987) *The Social Context of Criminal Justice Sentencing*, New York: Springer-Verlag.

Reynolds, H. T. (1977) *Analysis of Nominal Data*, Beverly Hills: Sage Publications.

Rosenberg, M. (1968) *The Logic of Survey Analysis.* New York: Basic Books.

Trigg, R. (1987) *Understanding Social Science.* Oxford: Basic Blackwell.

Wilbanks, William (1987) *The Myth of a Racist Criminal Justice System*, Brooks-Cole

SECTION II:

RACISM, EMPIRICISM and POLICY IMPLICATIONS

CHAPTER 9

Racial Discrimination in The Criminal Justice System:
Evidence from Four Jurisdictions

Michael J. Lynch/
E. Britt Patterson
Florida State University

Wilbanks' (1987) argument that no systematic race bias operates in the American criminal justice system has generated much controversy, yet appears to be gaining greater acceptance. We find this situation problematic given the methodological and definitional drawbacks of Wilbanks' work (see Lynch this volume; Ansari, this volume; Georges-Abeyie, this volume). For example, his definition and operationalization of race, and selective use of data all serve to bias the outcome in favor of a no discrimination finding (see Lynch, 1990). Thus, we feel that Wilbanks' conclusions concerning racial discrimination are, at best, premature.

In order to address the possibility of racial discrimination in the criminal justice system we examine the effects of victim/offender race interactions on judicial decision making at two points in the decision making process: decisions to incarcerate and length of sentence decisions. We do so based upon Black's (1976) assertion that the amount of law applied to individuals is the product of the vertical location of both the offender and the victim in social life. In Black's view, the amount of punishment applied to the offender is not solely a product of the offenders' characteristics; it also depends upon the characteristics of the victim as well. For example, black offenders who victimize whites are more likely to receive harsher sentences than blacks who victimize blacks (see e.g. Lafree 1989). In cases where the victim's status is greater than the offender's, punishment will be certain and severe. Conversely, where the victim occupies a lower status than the offender, punishment will be less certain and less severe (Black 1976:23-24). This notion is captured by Black as follows: "all else constant, lower ranks have less law than higher ranks" (1976:17).

Black's position has been supported by various studies. Myers and Hagan (1979), for instance, discovered that offenses against whites were more likely to be prosecuted than offenses against blacks; Paternoster (1984) found that prosecutors were more likely to charge black defendants who victimize white with capital offenses than other offender-victim combinations; Smith *et al*'s (1984) analysis revealed that police were less likely to make arrests in encounters involving black victims, but more likely to make arrests when the victim was white; and several studies (Parington 1965; Wolfgang and Reidel 1973; Zimring et al 1976; Bower and Pierce 1980) have demonstrated that blacks who victimize whites are more likely to be sentenced harshly than other racial combinations.

THEORETICAL BACKGROUND

Wilbanks conceptualizes racial discrimination as an 'all or nothing' phenomenon in which there is only one possible outcome: either (1) there is discrimination throughout the system (there is systematic bias, or DT), or (2) there is no systematic race bias across all decision making points in all jurisdictions (or NDT). There is, however, an alternative to this 'all or nothing' approach. This view, which we call the stage-related racial discrimination thesis (or SRRDT), claims that racial discrimination is systematic to the extent that it effects certain parts of the decision making process in a somewhat consistent (systematic) manner across jurisdictions. In short, all decisions may not be biased, but certain decisions may be consistently biased. This bias may be related to offender characteristics, or a combination of offender/victim characteristics.

The existence of bias at earlier decision making stages is problematic to the extent that once included at an early decision making stage, race-related bias continues to have an effect on latter-stage decisions, even if these associations are statistically suppressed.

METHODOLOGICAL LIMITATIONS

One of the principle reservations we have with Wilbanks' analysis concerns his operationalization of race. His black/white race distinction fails to capture the full extent of race discrimination by treating discrimination as a phenomenon that is related to being either black or white. This operationalization of race obscures racial discrimination to the extent that non-white minority groups are forced into the white race category (see Lynch this volume). Race issues are not, so to speak, black or white. In our view, a white/black race variable is not consistent with reality, and serves to compress race specific processing outcomes by inflating white race effects relative to black race effects by including other minority groups within the white race category. To counteract this tendency, we construct a more appropriate race variable: white/non-white.

In addition to using a different operationalization of race, the present study also focuses on victim/offender race interactions, or dyads, as a further test of DT, NDT and SRRDT perspectives. In short, racial discrimination may be exaggerated or attenuated depending upon the race of both the offender and the victim. This observation easily translates into three possible outcomes.

First, if NDT is correct, victim-offender race interactions should have no systematic effect on judicial decision making. Race, in this view, is not a decision making factor, and it should therefore make little difference if offenders and victims are from similar or dissimilar racial categories.

Second, the DT perspective predicts that non-white offenders who select or converge with white victims should be punished more severely (in our data, more likely to be sent to prison and more likely to receive longer prison sentences) than situations in which victims and offenders are of the same race. In other words, there should be a systematic race effect operating against non-whites who victimize whites across all decision making stages. Conversely, whites who victimize non-whites should receive the least amount of punishment. In short, not only does the offender's race affect decision making, but the victim's race might also be brought into play in a systematic manner at all decision making stages. Decision making is not based solely on the offender's race, but on the race of the victim as well (Black 1976).

Third, in our alternative, SRRDT, race-related bias against non-white offenders relative to white offenders (regardless of victim race) should be evident in early stages of the decision making process, but may not be evident at latter stages of decision making. This is so because at latter processing stages, only the most serious cases involving white offenders remain in the system. The race bias incorporated in early decision making stages is based primarily upon offender race.

DATA AND METHODS

The data for this analysis were drawn from Miller *et al*'s (1978) study of plea bargaining. This data contains processing information, and victim and offender information for six jurisdictions (New Orleans, Louisiana; Tucson, Arizona; Norfolk, Virginia; Seattle, Washington; El Paso, Texas and Delaware County, Pennsylvania). Data relating to El Paso and Delaware County were excluded from the present analysis due to extensive missing data for victim/offender relationships. In the remaining jurisdictions, approximately 85 percent of cases were robberies or burglaries, and thus we choose to concentrate on these two offense types. Further, white offender/non-white victim dyads were excluded from the analysis given the rarity of this type of interaction and problems associated with generating reliable estimates from small samples. After excluding non-burglary and robbery cases, white offender/non-white victim dyads, and eliminating Delaware County and El Paso, our final sample consists of 531 incarceration decisions and 289 length-of-sentence decisions for these four geographically diverse jurisdictions.

For the 531 incarceration decisions, all independent variables were treated as dichotomous variables, and logit estimation procedures were employed. Our model controls for the input of several legally relevant decision making variables (e.g. seriousness of the offense, number of witnesses, presence of physical evidence, prior arrests, and pre-trial detainment status) as well as extra-legal factors (age of victims relative to offenders, race of victim/offender, whether victims and offenders were strangers or acquainted, jurisdiction, and gender) that primarily represent victim/offender relationships.

FINDINGS AND DISCUSSION
INCARCERATION DECISIONS

A descriptive analysis of the 531 incarceration decisions, revealed that: (1) 67 percent of non-whites who victimized whites were incarcerated (N = 225); (2) 60 percent of non-white defendants who victimized non-whites were incarcerated (N = 146); (3) 35 percent of whites who victimized whites were incarcerated (N = 160); (4) inter-racial cases were more likely to result in sentences greater than one year than intra-racial cases; and (5) probation or incarceration for less than one year is a more likely form of punishment for white victim/offender dyads.

These findings indicate one of two possibilities at this stage of the analysis. First, non-white defendants, regardless of the race of the victim, are more likely to be sent to prison than white offenders. Second, whites victimized by white offenders receive less justice than white victims of non-white offenders. Neither of these findings provides full support for either the NDT or DT perspective, and have little bearing on SRRDT.

Our next step was to generate a multivariate logit estimation for these 531 incarceration decisions employing victim/offender race and 16 control variables (see Table 1). This procedure yielded ten statistically significant relationships (p < .05) that could be used to predict incarceration decisions: non-white offender/white victim (victim/offender race); type of offense; number of witnesses; presence of physical evidence; prior arrests; probation/parole at time of arrest;

Table 1:
Logit Estimates of Incarceration for Characteristics of Victim-Offender Dyads, Case Characteristics, Defendant Characteristics
(N = 531)

Variable	B	SE(B)	B/SE(B)	AP:P=.50
Both Victim and defendant nonwhite	.313	.303	1.033	.078
Non-white Defendant White Victim	.593*	.275	2.154	.144
Younger Victim	-.207	.336	-.617	-.052
Older Victim	-.133	.242	-.547	-.033
Male defendant Female Victim	-.135	.242	-.557	-.034
Victim and Defendant acquainted	-.009	.311	-.030	-.002
Harm to Victim	.074	.315	.234	.018
Robbery	1.191*	.270	4.110	.267
Number of Witnesses	.152*	.051	2.981	.038
Physical Evidence	1.016*	.308	3.303	.234
Prior Arrests	.171*	.053	3.231	.043
Probation/Parole at Arrest	.770*	.272	2.835	.184
Juvenile Record	.602*	.230	2.621	.146
Drug History	.792*	.275	2.876	.188
Pretrial Detainment	1.343*	.230	5.846	.293
New Orleans	.021	.416	.050	.005
Norfolk	-.081	.458	-.178	-.020
Seattle	-1.281*	.459	-2.791	-.283
Constant	-3.618			

$L^2 = 206.02$
Psuedo R^2 - .282   *significant at less than .05 level

juvenile record; drug history; and offender pre-trial detainment status. This logit estimation procedure demonstrates that the white victim/non-white offender dyad remains an important decision making factor when controlling for legally relevant decision making factors. This portion of the analysis provides some support for DT and SRRDT perspectives. Relative to white defendants and controlling for the effects of legally relevant criteria, type of crime and jurisdiction, non-white defendants who victimize whites are significantly more likely to receive a prison term than white defendants; however, non-whites who victimize other non-whites are not significantly more likely to be incarcerated than whites who have victimized other whites.

SENTENCE LENGTH ANALYSIS

As a further test of these three theoretical positions (DT, NDT, and SRRDT) we employed OLS estimation procedures to examine 289 length-of-incarceration decisions rendered in these four jurisdictions. If we examine the bivariate distribution between sentence length decisions and race (see Table 2), we note two outcomes: (1) twice as many (two-thirds) non-white defendants face sentence length decisions as compared to white defendants (one-third); and (2) average sentence length for white defendants is 20.5 months, and approximately 29 months for non-white defendants — or more than 40 percent higher for non-whites relative to whites.

Table 2:
Average Expected Sentence Length in Months by Characteristics of Victim-Offender Dyads (N = 289)

	Average Expected Sentence Length
RACE	
nonwhite defendant — white victim (149)	29.74
white defendant — white victim (54)	20.56
nonwhite defendant — nonwhite victim (86)	28.97
AGE	
victim older than defendant (144)	25.67
victim same age as defendant (102)	27.92
victim younger than defendant (43)	34.59
GENDER	
male defendant — male victim (204)	26.50
male defendant — female victim (85)	30.90
RELATIONAL DISTANCE	
defendant a stranger to victim (246)	27.98
defendant acquainted with victim (43)	26.74

Multivariate OLS estimates, however, indicate that victim/offender race relationships are not statistically significant at the sentence length stage of decision making (see Table 3). This finding appears to favor the NDT approach, given that a systematic race bias is not noted in every step of the judicial decision making process across these jurisdictions. At the sentence length decision making stage only legally relevant and jurisdictional control measures are statistically associated with sentence length (*i.e.* seriousness of offense, number of witnesses, prior arrests, on probation/parole at time of arrest, pretrial detainment status, plead guilty, and whether the offense was tried in Norfolk or Seattle). However, two methodological deficiencies cause us to have reservations concerning the findings of the OLS estimates.

First, since we control for victim/offender relationship and not simply offender race in this analysis, offender race might still have an unmeasured effect on sentence length (as evident in univariate portion of the analysis). In short, while we find no discrimination in relation to victim/offender race interaction, we have not ruled out or controlled for the effect, if any, of offender race alone.

Second, a no discrimination finding at this late stage of judicial making can be attributed to sample selection bias incorporated in sentence length decision making through earlier race-related decision making processes (e.g. in these data, the decision to incarcerate). In other words, the sample of defendants reaching the sentence length decision stage are not a representative or random sample of all defendants. This pool of defendants has been chosen according to specific, non-random (and extra-legal) criteria, and part of this criteria was victim/offender race interactions. As a result, such data has limited validity when assessing race discrimination at this late stage of judicial making.

Table 3:
Ols Estimates of Log of Average Expected Sentence for Characteristics of Victim-Offender Dyads, Case and Defendant Characteristics (N = 289)

	B	SE(B)
Both victim and defendant non-white	.232	.160
Nonwhite defendant white victim	.101	.146
Younger victim	.179	.159
Older victim	-.115	.113
Male defendant female victim	-.046	.112
Victim and defendant acquainted	-.178	.155
Harm to victim	.140	.136
Robbery	.352*	.118
Number of witnesses	.064*	.023
Prior arrests	.078*	.023
Probation/parole at arrest	.295*	.117
Pretrial detainment	.305*	.125
Plead	-.330*	.136
New Orleans	.314	.210
Norfolk	.811*	.229
Seattle	.635*	.245
Constant	1.507	
R^2		.292

*significant less than .05 level

Given the evidence reported in this analysis, we continue to have reservations regarding the validity of NDT. We have not ruled out, and in fact have found some support for SRRDT. Furthermore, the evidence of differential effects of race at different stages of the decision making process can be explained by an alternative, equally plausible position. Evidence of non-racial discrimination in sentencing length cannot be taken as evidence of NDT due to confounding factors related to offense seriousness, the finding that race discrimination exists at earlier processing stages (outside of the problem of sample selection bias), and the fact that this bias relates to victim/offender interactions, not simply the offender's race. We believe that early processing stages weed out the least serious crimes involving white defendants, but not those involving non-white defendants. As a result, only the most serious cases involving white defendants reach the sentencing decision stage, while the same cannot be said for non-white defendants.

In order to fully test an NDT, probability estimates for individual cases across several criminal justice decision making points using tobit, logit or probit procedures need to be employed. These statistical procedures allow researchers to test whether decisions rendered at each processing stage contain a bias, and using appropriate controls, measure whether the outcomes at one stage are related to the outcomes at earlier stages. Until such research is conducted, closure on the NDT/DT debate cannot be reached empirically, and will continue to be based on conjecture.

CONCLUSIONS

In sum, our data and theory suggest that neither a DT or NDT position provides a completely accurate picture of racial discrimination in criminal justice processes. Both positions represent extremes of the racial discrimination argument. DT implies that racial discrimination is systematic or evident at every stage of the criminal justice process; NDT argues that even if racial discrimination is evident at certain stages of criminal processing, its absence at other stages suggest that there is no systematic evidence of race discrimination. Given the data, and the theoretical and definitional problems evident in the literature assessing this issue (especially NDT literature), neither position can be fully supported. In fact, we believe that the truth concerning race discrimination lies somewhere in between these two interpretations: racial bias is clearly evident at certain stages of criminal justice decision making, and the decisions rendered at later stages depend upon these biases. Thus, while later stage decisions may not demonstrate a statistically significant race relationship, these decisions are indeed contaminated by earlier, racially related decisions.

Finally, statistical studies of processing and racism fail to fully explore the extent of racism through its neglect of qualitative aspects of discrimination (see George-Abeyie, this volume). These range from informal, unmeasured processes that operate against non-white offenders, to language barriers, failure to comprehend legal rules and procedures, availability of quality legal representation, and even the race biases incorporated in legal decision making criteria. Until all these aspects are comprehensively analyzed, it is a mistake to operate under the assumption that the criminal justice system is not racially biased, especially in light of other biases (e.g. social class) for which we have evidence (see Wilbanks 1987; Reiman 1990; Lynch and Groves 1989).

REFERENCES

Ansari, Z. reference to this volume

Black, D. (1976) *The Behavior of Law*, N.Y.: Academic Press.

Bowers, W.J. and G.G.Pierce, (1980) "Arbitrariness and Discrimination in Past-Furman and Capital Cases" *Crime and Delinquency* 26:563-635.

Georges-Abeyie, D., reference to this volume

Lafree, G. (1989) *Rape and Criminal Justice*, Belmont, CA: Wadsworth.

Lynch, M. J (1990)., Reference to this volume

Lynch, Michael J. and W. Byron Groves (1989) *Primer in Radical Criminology*, N.Y.: Harrow and Heston.

Myers, M.A. and J.Hagan (1979) "Private and Public Trouble: Prosecutors and the Allocation of Court Resources" *Social Problems* 28:246-262.

Parington, D. (1965) "The Incidence of the death Penalty for Rape in Virginia" *Washington and Lee Law Review* 22:43-75.

Paternoster, R. (1984) "Prosecutorial Discretion in Requesting the Death Penalty: A Case of Victim Based Racial Discrimination" *Law and Society Review* 18:437-478.

Reiman, Jeffrey (1990) *The Rich get Richer and the Poor get Prison* N.Y.: Wiley.

Smith, D.A., C.A. Visher, and L.A. Davidson (1984) "Equity and Discretionary Justice: The Influence of Race on Police Arrest Decisions" *Journal of Criminal Law and Criminology* 75:234-249.

Wolfgang, M.E. and M. Reidel (1973) "Race, Judicial Discretion and the Death Penalty" *The Annals of the American Academy of Political and Social Science* 407:119-133.

Zimring, F.E., J. Eigen and S. O'Malley (197) "Punishing Homicide in Philadelphia: Perspectives on the Death Penalty" *University of Chicago Law Review* 43:227-252.

CHAPTER 10

Discrimination Against Native Peoples in The Canadian Parole Process

W. S. DeKeseredy / B. D. MacLean

"Law and justice are distant relatives. And in [this country], they are not even on speaking terms." [1]

INTRODUCTION

That all data are inaccurate and inhere some degree of measurement error is a truism which applies unequivocally to official statistics of all varieties. Census data, perhaps the best available, are wrought with missing cases, unanswered questions, poorly worded questions, questions which are answered incorrectly, wrong information, lies and computational errors. Health care data contain wrong diagnoses, incorrect billing codes, computational errors, and a host of errors which are derived from the human errors in recording these data. Despite these errors, official statistics are readily used in an uncritical way by social scientists who, by the merits of their training, recognize the deficiencies; nevertheless, they proceed to use these data as if they were perfectly accurate, and draw unqualified conclusions as if they were truths.

Of the many kinds of official statistics, criminal justice data are, perhaps, the worst in terms of the errors they include and the ways in which they are misused. Often, these data are used as indicators for the frequency and distribution of crime despite the fact that anyone who knows anything at all about basic issues in criminology recognizes that the statistics tell us more about the system that compiles them (Downes and Rock, 1984) than they do about actual patterns and variations of crime (MacLean, 1989). As far back as 1911, Robinson observed that the best statistics would be those collected by the judiciary, not the police, and in 1931, Sellin argued that the further from the source of the crime that the recording takes place, the less accurate will be the data (Maltz, 1977).

The debate concerning the accuracy of official crime statistics, then, has been raging on for a long time beginning with writers such as Comte and Quetelet (Bierne, 1987) and reaching a plateau with the Wickersham Commission of 1931 (Maltz, 1977). Maltz (1977) points out that the Uniform Crime Reports (UCR) were adopted in 1930 by J. Edgar Hoover, without proper legislative authority, after being recommended by the International Association of Chiefs of Police (IACP) in 1929. The reason that Hoover so quickly and inappropriately adopted the UCR was not because of their ability to explain, predict and control crime (although this is certainly what he argued); rather, he recognized their utility as a device for managing both the police force and the public perceptions of the police force (MacLean, 1989). The 1931 Wickersham Commission was strongly critical of Hoover's early political manipulation of the UCR, and in their report, warned about the potential misuse of such data:

> For purposes of a check upon the different agencies of criminal justice it is important that the compiling and publication of statistics should not be confided to any one bureau or agency which is engaged in administering the criminal law. It takes but little experience of such criminal statistics as we have in order to convince that a serious abuse exists in compiling them as a basis for requesting appropriations or for justifying the existence of or urging expanded powers and equipment for the agency in power [2].

Thus, far from being seen as accurate, even government agencies, in concert with criminologists and academics, concede that official crime statistics are not good indicators of the frequency and distribution of crime, with citations too numerous to mention. [3]

If the debate concerning official crime data reached a plateau in 1931, the intensity of the debate was heightened during the 1960s (Phipps, 1987) when the historical advance represented by the phenomenological revolution and the emergence of the labelling tradition completely debunked the positivist paradigm by relentlessly attacking its empirical basis: official crime statistics (MacLean, 1989). Indeed, seminal works by Kitsuse and Cicourel (1963) and Bell (1962) not only argued that official data were inaccurate, but were so successful in challenging the positivist paradigm that it was quickly displaced as the dominant mode of criminological discourse and replaced by a more critical line of inquiry from which sprang voluminous writings packed with keen criminological insight.

However, if the positivists were displaced, they rebounded with an entirely new methodology and empirical basis: the victimization study. In the recognition that the arguments against official data were far too strong to be countered, positivist empiricists required a new source of information from which to estimate the frequency and distribution of crime, and for this they turned to large-scale probability surveys of crime victims (Sparks,1982). Beginning with the Presidential Commission on Law Enforcement and The Administration of Justice (1967), this 'neo-positivist' approach to studying crime was launched[4], and on the surface, was so successful in moving beyond some of the limitations of official crime statistics, that in 1972 financial commitments were undertaken for the National Crime Survey (NCS) that cost the U.S. taxpayer a total of $53 million between 1972 and 1977 (U.S. House of Representatives, 1977).

Now that there are nearly 20 years of NCS data in the U.S. combined with reams of similar studies funded at an astronomical expense by virtually every government in the Western world, we find it absolutely inconceivable that anyone flirting with the identity of 'scientist', could be so stubbornly optimistic and so stubbornly empirical as to actually argue that official crime statistics are in any way an accurate reflection of the actual frequency and distribution of offense patterns in society. Nevertheless, there are some who are that stubborn. For example, Mawby (1979) argues that while official crime statistics under-report actual criminal frequencies, they do so in proportions which are accurate reflections of the distribution of crime within particular jurisdictions.[5] Of more relevance, here, however, is the stubbornly empirical analysis advanced by Wilbanks.

Our purpose in writing this essay is twofold. Firstly, we provide a brief critique of Wilbanks' work and argue that, despite his claims to the contrary, it must be viewed as biased and unscientific. In order to illustrate this point, we will look to some recent developments in the treatment of Native peoples in the Canadian parole process. We will demonstrate that given Wilbanks' own criteria, the criminal justice system in Canada *is* the embodiment of racial discrimination, particularly in its treatment of Native people.

WILBANKS: THE VEIL OF SOCIAL SCIENTIFIC OBJECTIVITY

We argue that the basis of Wilbanks' analysis can be summarized as follows: 1) blacks are disproportionately represented in the criminal justice system; 2) after analyzing both official data and NCS data from two jurisdictions, Wilbanks concludes that blacks offend at a rate higher than whites; 3) in California the black/white gap increases from arrest to prison, while in Pennsylvania it decreases; 4) thus, blacks are over-represented because they exhibit higher levels of criminality, and to the extent that this over-representation is in excess of their higher levels of criminality in some jurisdictions, it is lower in others. Therefore, the justice system is not racist overall; rather, it reflects higher levels of black offending *vis à vis* whites. At some points blacks are treated more harshly, at others more leniently. Where it exists, the unfairness is random and cancels out overall.

With regard to the first point, it is clear that blacks are over-represented in the system of social control and we find this observation unproblematic; however, how this discrepancy is to be explained is a matter of debate. In our view, there are really only two possibilities: either blacks have a higher level of criminality or the system is racist (or a combination of both). Wilbanks appears to side with the former. Clearly, there are elements of both operant here of which Wilbanks is not cognizant. He errs by assuming that categories of 'offending' are unproblematic, a robbery is a robbery regardless of who commits it and regardless of who observes it.

With reference to point two, Wilbanks assumes that blacks have a higher level of criminality. Despite his claims of objectivity, he sorts out his ideology first and he then goes out to prove it is correct. Such political posturing is hardly scientific. He errs by using official categories and official data early in his analysis as if these were unproblematic. He then proceeds to use NCS data to test his thesis later in his analysis. This contradiction is weakly justified by the argument that because of the deficiencies of official crime data, particularly under-reporting, NCS data are more appropriate. Wilbanks fails to consider that the NCS is a victimization survey, not a self-report offense study. For this reason, therefore, he relies upon the observations of the untrained victim rather than the observations of the trained police officer inherent in an official crime statistics data base.

Wilbanks might be as objective as he claims in using this data source. If that is the case then he is clearly confused, contradictory and lacking intellectual insight. On page 23 of this volume he states that: "*I fail to see how anyone can claim that statistical evidence is more subject to bias than observations.*" Well, Dr. Wilbanks, it is this *blindness* which invalidates your entire argument — for what are statistics and statistical evidence if they are not observations? Like all social phenomena, statistics are not naturally existing, God-given categories; they are constructed socially. They are both the product of observation and the categories within which observations are framed. Good social scientists recognize this problem when studying reality and make the conscious effort not to bring their ethno-centric categories to the study. Rather the scientific strategy is to glean the appropriate categories from the reality being studied. Instead, Wilbanks draws on the observations of non-social-scientific respondents. Wilbanks might benefit from a careful reading of left realist literature which articulates the conservative biases inherent in NCS data.

There are two other difficulties in using crime survey data for this purpose. Firstly, as Skogan (1981) points out, to measure criminal 'incidents' is to conceptualize discrete moments in a process. From this we can say that crime is a process (MacLean, 1986), and to focus only upon discrete moments within that process which are defined by a particular set of ideological categories is not science but reified scientific ideology.

Finally, Wilbanks is implicitly arguing that statistical techniques are objective not biased. In order for this assertion to be correct, there are two assumptions which cannot be violated. Firstly, one must assume that the categories being used are objective in their construction and that they are appropriate to the reality. This assumption is not warranted because the materials from which legal discourse is constructed are male, white and bourgeois.[6] Secondly, one must assume that there are no measurement errors, an assumption which is ludicrous — there are always measurement errors, particularly in survey research. Wilbanks violates this assumption by default in refusing to recognize measurement error. Thus his arguments are both fallacious and unscientific because they are not falsifiable.

The tendency for dealing with this basic limitation of crime survey research is to mystify the data with tests of statistical analysis. In this way the analysis appears precise and scientific, when, in fact, tests of statistical significance ignore measurement error. Indeed, these are tests of sampling error. On this point Sparks (1982) has made it perfectly clear that for crime survey research, it is not sampling error which presents the problem but measurement error. If Wilbanks were aware of this literature, he might be more reluctant to make claims about his superior accuracy and objectivity.

Given these problems, the balance of Wilbanks' logic does not follow and his entire argument is invalidated; however, his work is not a total loss. He makes the observation that one indicator of systematic racism would be disparity across the various decision making points of the justice process. To this we would add that while such disparity is sufficient to indicate racism, is not a necessary condition to establish racism. While Wilbanks argues that there is no evidence to support this contention in the U.S., we argue that such a condition is characteristic of Canadian criminal justice. In the section which follows we will illustrate this disparity with an examination of the way in which Native peoples fare in the parole decision making process.

NATIVES AND THE PAROLE PROCESS IN CANADA

According to MacLean and Ratner (1987) the development of parole in Canada proceeded through a series of stages. Prior to the Ticket of Leave Act (1899) (TOL), the Royal Prerogative of Mercy was the only form of early release and represented an act of clemency; however, with the passing of TOL, a new correctional ideology of rehabilitation was introduced. Also in existence was good conduct remission, another form of early release. The authors argue that for Native peoples (Indians, Métis and Innuit), 'rehabilitation' meant adopting white middle class values outside the prison and that 'good conduct' meant a similar adoption inside the prison. Unfortunately, the 'objectivity' of statistical data cannot confirm this because as Goldenberg, Chair of the Standing Senate Committee on Legal and Constitutional Affairs, states in his report on parole in Canada:

> This report has made little use of statistics on parole because the information is inadequate. It is not reliable enough to give even accurate headcounts. It neither permits actual statistical descriptions nor, meaningful assessments of various programs (1974:125).

In 1959, the *Parole Act* was introduced in Canada after being recommended by The Fateux Committee (1956), and the National Parole Board was formed with the authority to implement the *Act*. Again, the officially-stated purpose of parole was for rehabilitation. Thus, underlying parole in Canada is the same correctionalist ideology to which Wilbanks subscribes in his work.

In his inquiry into corrections in Canada, Ouimet (1969) makes the observation that those prisoners to whom full parole is granted represent the least risk, while those not granted parole, represent the highest risk for re-offending. Thus, the ironic effect of parole is that the low risks are released into the community under supervision, while those who are deemed to be the high risks are eventually released into the community without any supervision. This observation led to amendments to the *Parole Act* in 1970 in which all prisoners were required to spend the portion of their sentence which represented good conduct remission under mandatory supervision on the street. While the intention was to ensure that higher risk prisoners were released under supervision, the result was that, in many instances, those whose post-release plans were considered to be inadequate were denied full parole and forced to stay incarcerated until their release under mandatory supervision. That Native peoples were disproportionately disadvantaged here is proven from a number of sources. Demers (1978) finds that Native peoples have a lower full-parole release rate than white prisoners, which means that there is a greater gap at the point of mandatory supervision — i.e. Native peoples are more likely to be denied parole and to be under mandatory supervision status. The Solicitor General's Working Group on parole argues:

> Native offenders have a lower full parole release rate and a higher revocation rate than the population as a whole...This is not an indicator of racism in corrections, but in many cases reflects a lack of release plans considered appropriate by releasing authorities (1981:117).

The Federation of Saskatchewan Indians sees this judgement of Native offenders' release plans as a form of discrimination. In their brief to the Goldenberg Committee they argue:

> the Indian parolee was obliged to tailor his parole plan in order to meet the supervision requirements regardless of whether or not his preference lay in returning to the reserve. With a move to the city, often came a burden of general cultural adjustment, the stigma of a criminal coupled with the pressures of prejudice and discrimination because of his *Indianness*, and the culturally based problems in communication between himself and his non-Indian parole supervisor. (1973:20).

Perhaps, this discrimination is best illustrated by the Solicitor General's (1981) ten-year study of mandatory parole in which an entire two paragraphs of a 155 page report are devoted to Native offenders as a *Special Offender Group*. Thus, while the Solicitor General sees native offenders as a special case, they are a case not worthy of much consideration, except of course in the decision of whether or not to grant parole. As MacLean and Ratner argue, the use of this category means that Native people are singled out for special treatment; however, this distinction is a negative one not a positive one because it means that Native parolees have a greater number of technical restrictions attached to their release which, if violated, mean suspension of parole status and return to prison, *even if no new crime is committed.*

In order to illustrtate this data from the 1981 Solicitor General study can be used. This study shows that during the first ten years of mandatory supervision, the proportion of parolee revocations due to the commission of a new offence drops from 33% of all those released to 14.6% in 1979. Conversely, the proportion of those revoked without committing a new offence rises from 0% in 1970 to 19.4% in 1979. Thus more parolees are being returned without even violating the law, and since Native peoples are already over-represented in this group, and because Native peoples have more special restrictions than their white counterparts, the Native success rate on parole is reduced. When this disparity is understood by decision-makers as a higher level of criminality in the Native population (despite the fact that no crime has been committed), then the stereotype of 'greater risk' is reproduced, and serves to disadvantage the Native offender even more in terms of positive decisions in the parole process. Thus, when we examine the phenomenon as a process, rather than as a series of discrete moments, we can observe that what appears as a higher level of criminality is an artifact which is structured by discriminatory decision-making practices. If we were to proceed from this point, as Wilbanks does, then we would come to the conclusion that the over-representation of Native peoples in the groups being denied parole and having parole revoked is representative of higher levels of criminality. In reality, however, the conception of higher criminality is the product of racist observations resulting in racist decisions which are reflected in the "objective empirical data". No doubt, were Wilbanks to employ his method of analysis on South African data he would have to conclude that the criminal justice system in that country is not racist either.

The final evidence for discrimination comes from the period after 1986. In July 1986, Canadian Parliament passed Bills C-67 and C-68 which give the National Parole Board the authority *to deny mandatory supervision*. After the first year of operation 60% of the detainees under these *acts* were native peoples (MacLean and Ratner, 1987). Thus we see a higher disproportion of Native peoples at each decision point and at each level of severity of treatment:

> While Native peoples represent only 2.04 percent of the Canadian population, they constitute almost one third of the prison population on the Prairies and are almost twice that proportion again among those who are referred for detention under Bill C-67.... at each stage of severity of treatment, Native prisoners are increasingly over-represented. Senator Earl Hastings, a self-appointed watchdog of the prison system, carried out his own investigation... After visiting all but two of the detainees, he concluded that: "The sad part is most of them are Native Boys with no knowledge of what is going on or the evidence against them." (MacLean and Ratner , 1987:55).

Thus using Wilbanks' own criteria there is sufficient evidence to show that the Canadian criminal justice process discriminates against Native peoples. Perhaps, if Wilbanks were not so rigid in his thinking, he might find that in processual terms, non-white minorities are disadvantaged by one of the most racist sets of organized state practices in the Western World — the U.S. Criminal Justice System.

ENDNOTES

1. Line spoken by Marlon Brando in his role as a South African Civil Rights Lawyer in the recent film entitled: *A Dry White Season.*.
2. Wickersham Commission (1931), cited in Maltz (1977).
3. For a brief discussion of the limitations of official crime data and a review of literature pertaining to these see: MacLean, 1986.
4. According to Sparks (1982) it was Inkeri Antilla who conducted the first victimization survey by mail in Finland in 1964.
5. For qualification of Mawby's view, see: Lowman, 1982; Mawby, 1989; Lowman, 1991.
6. For a good discussion see the recent issue of *Social Justice* (Headley, 1989).

REFERENCES

Bell, D. (1962) "The Myth of Crime Waves" D. Bell (ed.) *The End of Ideology: On The Exhaustion of Political Ideas in The Fifties*, New York: Free Press:137-158

Bierne, P. (1987) "Adolphe Quetelet and The Origins of Positivist Criminology" *American Journal of Sociology*, 29 (5):1140-69.

Demers, D. (1978) *Discretion, Disparity and The Parole Process*, Edmonton: Unpublished doctoral dissertation, University of Alberta.

Downes, D. and P. Rock (1984/82) *Understanding Deviance*, Oxford:Clarendon.

Federation of Saskatchewan Indians (1973) *Brief to the Standing Committee on Legal and Constitutional Affairs*, Ottawa: Information Canada.

Fateux, Justice (Chair) (1956) *Report of a Committee To Inquire Into The Principles and Practices Followed in The Remission Service of The Department of Justice of Canada*, Ottawa: Queen's Printer.

Goldenberg, C. (Chair) (1974) *Parole in Canada: Report of the Standing Committee on Legal and Constitutional Affairs*, Ottawa: Information Canada.

Headley, B. (Guest ed.) (1989) *Racism, Powerlessness, and Justice*, special ed. *Social Justice* 16 (4).

Kitsuse, J. and A. Cicourel (1963) "A Note on the Use of Official Crime Statistics" *Social Problems*, 11:131-139.

Lowman, J. (1982) "Crime, Criminal Justice Policy and The Urban Environment" D.P. Herbert and R. J. Johnston (eds.) *Geography and The Urban Environment* , Vol. 5, Chichester: Wiley: 307-342.

Lowman, J. (1991) "Police Practices and Crime Rates" D. J. Evans, D.T. Herbert and N. Fyfe (eds.) *Geography and Policing: New Spatial Perspectives* , London: Routledge

MacLean, B. D. "Critical Criminology and Some Limitations of Traditional Inquiry" B.D. MacLean (ed) *The Political Economy of Crime:* Toronto:Prentice-Hall Inc.:1-20.

MacLean, B. D. (1989a) *The Islington Crime Survey 1985: A Cross-Sectional Study of Crime and Policing in The London Borough of Islington*, London: Unpublished doctoral dissertation, London School of Economics and Political Science.

MacLean, B. and R. Ratner (1987) "An Historical Analysis of Bills C-67 and C-68: Implications for The Native Offender" *Native Studies Review*, 3 (1): 31-58.

Maltz, M. (1977) "Crime Statistics: A Historical Perspective" *Crime and Delinquency*, Jan.:32-40.

Mawby, R. (1979) *Policing The City*, Farnborough: Saxon House.

Mawby, R. (1989) "Policing and The Criminal Area" D.J. Evans and D. T. Herbert, (eds.) *The Geography of Crime*, London: Routledge: 260-281.

Ouimet, R. (1969) *Report of The Canadian Committee on Corrections: Toward Unity: Criminal Justice and Corrections*, Ottawa: Information Canada.

Phipps, A. (1987) *Criminal Victimization, Crime Control and Political Action*, London: Unpublished doctoral dissertation, Middlesesx Polytechnic.

Robinson, L. (1911) *History and Organization of Criminal Statistics in The United States*, Boston:Houghton Mifflin.

Sellin, T. (1931) "The Basis of a Crime Index" *Journal of Criminal Law and Criminology*, 22:335-336.

Skogan, W. (1981) *Issues in The Measurement of Victimization*, Washington, D.C.: U.S.G.P.O.

Solicitor General of Canada (1981) *Report of The Working Group, Solicitor General's Study of Conditional Release*, Ottawa: Supply and Services.

Sparks, R. (1982) *Research on Victims of Crime: Accomplishments, Issues and New Directions*, Rockville, MD: DHSS.

U.S. House of Representatives (1977) *Suspension of The National Crime Survey*, Washington, D.C.: U.S.G.P.O.

CHAPTER 11

Reaction To McCleskey vs Georgia

William Wilbanks
Florida International University

In 1972, the U.S. Supreme Court struck down all state capital punishment laws on the ground that death was being 'wantonly' and 'freakishly' imposed. The majority opinion suggested the death penalty might still be constitutional if state law provided for 'guided' discretion. In response, several states passed legislation that restricted the death penalty to certain kinds of premeditated murder, provided for guidance to judges and juries through lists of acceptable aggravating and mitigating factors, and required automatic appellate review to determine if the death sentence was 'excessive' given similar cases.

In 1976, the U.S. Supreme Court upheld the state death penalty statutes (in Georgia, Texas and Florida) that provided statutory criteria for the imposition of the death penalty and appellate review for proportionality. The Court expressed the view that the guidelines and appellate review would eliminate or reduce the arbitrariness in the imposition of the death penalty so that such factors as race would not play a determining role in the imposition of the death penalty. But the ruling of the Supreme Court was based on *theory* rather than *practice* in that it was assumed or theorized (in the absence of data) that guidelines and review would reduce discretion and discrimination.

The *theory* of the Court spurred numerous researchers to examine the *practice* of those states whose death penalty laws were approved by the court. A number of statistical studies have been published in recent years that challenge the optimistic view of the U.S. Supreme Court that arbitrariness and discrimination in the imposition of the death penalty could be significantly reduced by guidelines and review.

On April 22, 1987, the U.S. Supreme Court, in a 5-4 vote, upheld the conviction of a black man, Warren McCleskey, who shot and killed a white police officer in a 1978 Atlanta furniture store robbery. Lawyers for McCleskey had claimed that he was the victim of a system that tends to impose the death sentence on those who murder whites disproportionately more often than on people convicted of killing blacks. Many constitutional scholars believe that the McCleskey decision was the last broad challenge to the death penalty that could have affected hundreds of death-row cases nationwide. The U.S. Supreme Court clearly refused to abolish the death penalty and thus future challenges are likely to be restricted to issues limited to a single case.

The most controversial part of the Mccleskey decision was the rejection by the Court of the conclusions (of racial bias by race of victim) of a statistical study by David Baldus (and colleagues), a University of Iowa law professor. Baldus' study of almost 2,500 homicide cases in Georgia from 1973 to 1979 indicated that those who killed white victims were 11 times as likely to be given the death penalty as those who killed blacks. Furthermore, the Court majority ruled that McCleskey would have to prove direct racial discrimination in his case rather than infer discrimination in Georgia, via statistics (e.g., the Baldus study), in other cases.

The Supreme Court's decision in McCleskey has been strongly criticized by many in the research/academic community and the media. An example of this criticism is seen in the lead paragraph of a syndicated column by Anthony Lewis on the McCleskey decision:

> Confronted with powerful evidence that racial feelings play a large part in determining who will live and who will die, the U.S. Supreme Court closed its eyes. It effectively condoned the expression of racism in a profound aspect of our law.

The purpose of this paper is to both defend and criticize the McCleskey ruling — it is, as the title implies, "Reaction to *McCleskey* vs. *Georgia*."

FIRST, critics of the Court ruling have either misread or purposely distorted the majority opinion by Justice Powell. The Court did not "accept the validity of the (Baldus) study" in the sense suggested by critics. A close reading of the majority opinion by Justice Lewis Powell clearly indicates that the Court viewed the Baldus study as only indicative of a correlation between race of victim and the death penalty — not necessarily a race bias. Powell wrote that *even if* the *statistics* were valid the *conclusion* by Baldus (*i.e.*, that there was a race bias, not simply a correlation between race and outcome) did not necessarily follow. The Powell opinion stated that "at most, the Baldus study indicated a discrepancy that appears to correlate with race."

But critics have left the erroneous impression that the majority opinion upheld the Georgia death penalty even though it acknowledged that racial discrimination had been clearly proven in the Baldus study. This distortion of the Court ruling is strategic in that it places the Court (and its supporters) in the untenable position of upholding the death penalty in spite of clear proof of racism in its imposition. However, this misreading of the ruling is partly the fault of a poorly worded opinion by Justice Powell where language such as "we assume the validity of the statistics" could be easily misinterpreted if not read in context of the entire opinion. The media can be excused for misinterpreting the opinion given the wording utilized by the Court. But, in my view, academic critics of the decision have purposely distorted the ruling in order to portray the Court majority as being unconcerned about racism.

SECOND, the Supreme Court should be criticized for failing to grapple with the evidence presented in Baldus. It should be noted that the Baldus study was found to be seriously flawed by the U.S. District Court which first considered the statistical 'proof' presented for McCleskey via Baldus. After hearing the evidence from statisticians from both sides, the District Court judge ruled that "the data base has substantial flaws" and that McCleskey "failed to establish by a preponderance of the evidence that it is essentially trustworthy." The Judge pointed out that the greater likelihood of receiving death if the victim were white rather than black was reduced from 11:1 to 4.3:1 when *some* factors (e.g., whether the defendant was offered a plea bargain) that might have further reduced the 4.3:1 disparity were not utilized. Clearly, the Federal District Court judge did not see Baldus study as 'proof' of racial discrimination.

The U.S. Court of Appeals and the U.S. Supreme Court failed to rule on the District Court's evaluation of the Baldus study. Perhaps they were 'scared off' by the specter of a federal judge, who was clearly an amateur in statistics and methodology, 'refereeing' an argument among prominent statisticians. The briefs filed for McCleskey clearly pointed out some of the errors in fact and interpretation of the District Judge. It is likely that the two higher courts decided they were not going to get involved in a statistical quagmire — they would simply bypass the statistical evidence and base their ruling on other grounds (e.g., that no discrimination had been suggested or proven in McCleskey's case).

That decision was, in my view, a 'cop-out' and a mistake. I believe the proper course of action (as suggested by two of the Justices) was to remand the case to the Court of Appeals for a ruling on the validity of the Baldus study's methods and conclusions. The court should have directly confronted the evidence in Baldus rather than to just suggest that the study was indicative of a correlation only, and not a race effect. The Court did not fully explain why the Baldus study did not prove what it claimed to prove — it only rejected the *conclusion* of Baldus while conceding that the *statistics* of Baldus were valid. The Supreme Court thus said, on one hand, that it would not rule on the validity of the Baldus study, while at the same time it adopted the District Court's (and the State's) position that the conclusion (of a race effect) of the study was unjustified. Thus the Supreme Court implicitly adopted the conclusion of the District Court without getting into a statistical debate.

The Supreme Court, perhaps realizing that it had accepted the State's contention that Baldus did not prove a 'race effect' while refusing to grapple with the data and methodology of the study to explain its rejection of the Baldus conclusions, then presented a 'back-up position'. Powell suggested that even if one could prove (which they claimed Baldus did not) a race effect in 'other cases', there was no evidence of direct racial discrimination in McCleskey's case. It is as if the Court was trying to end what might become an endless statistical debate by ruling on the death penalty in a way that would eliminate the possibility of some later statistical study overcoming the defects pointed out by the District Court. Thus the Court was saying, in effect, "Let's end this debate over the death penalty, let's rule in a way that will preclude future challenges based on statistical evidence."

Unfortunately, the decision to require proof of direct discrimination in a particular case flies in the face of prior decisions and establishes a burden that will be difficult, if not impossible, to meet. How can anyone prove that discrimination occurred in a particular case unless someone admits to making a decision based on race? This standard has not been imposed in other spheres such as in employment discrimination and jury discrimination so it is difficult to see why such a stringent standard should be applied in death penalty cases.

THIRD, it appears that the over-riding concern of the Court majority was to preserve the death penalty process and the criminal justice system against constitutional challenges based on disparity in outcome by race (or some other illegitimate factor). This desire led the court to 'create' the new Constitutional burden of having to prove direct discrimination in a particular case rather than allowing discrimination in a system to be inferred from statistical data. The Powell opinion made it clear that if the Court agreed with McCleskey that race of victim was a determinant in outcome and thus invalidated the Georgia death penalty system, a whole series of challenges would follow.

The court specifically mentioned the sex factor. Though males are arrested at a ratio of approximately 7 to 1 compared to females, males outnumber females on death row by approximately 82 to 1. Thus the death penalty system in the U.S. appears to favor females over males at a ratio of over 11 to 1. All male killers would argue that, given the ruling in McCleskey, their conviction and/or sentence should be overturned since female killers are treated more leniently.

And if the death penalty process, with all of its statutory guidelines and safeguards, is overturned there is the likelihood that non-capital sentences would be even more likely infected with illegitimate disparities in outcomes and thus subject to constitutional challenge. The court decided that the best way to end such challenges was to reject evidence of inferred racism via statistical evidence and thereby eliminate similar claims for sexism, and so forth.

FOURTH, there are grounds to reject the conclusions of Balbus if that study were directly confronted by the court. Baldus concluded that racism permeated the Georgia death penalty system in that those who killed white rather than black victims were more likely to receive the death penalty. Thus racism is inferred in decision-makers (e.g., prosecutors, juries) in the Georgia system from the race of victim disparities presented by Baldus. This 'theory' by Baldus implicitly suggests that white decision-makers exercised racial discrimination against blacks by devaluing black life via leniency to those who killed blacks rather than whites. And yet Baldus presented no evidence on a critical variable — the race of prosecutors and juries. We do not know how many prosecutors involved in the Georgia cases were white *vs.* black nor do we know the extent to which all-white or bi-racial juries voted for the death penalty in the cases studied by Baldus. The Supreme Court could have refused to invalidate the death penalty in Georgia solely on the failure to establish that the 'accusers' (e.g., white prosecutors and jurors) were in fact white (as implicitly suggested by Baldus).

There has been much discussion about how the Baldus study controlled for over 200 variables and yet still found a race of victim disparity. The great number of control variables is a smokescreen in that it is seldom mentioned that the factors considered most important by the actual decision-makers (e.g., prosecutors) and critics of the death penalty were not utilized as controls. If prosecutors are asked what factors most influence their decision to seek a death penalty they will mention strength of evidence, whether the jury was likely to convict, and whether the defendant was willing to accept a plea bargain (McCleskey was not willing to plead). None of these factors were measured by Baldus. Furthermore, critics of the death penalty system often suggest that the bias of all-white juries is one of the greatest dangers in the system. And yet the Baldus study did not control for race of jurors. What if all-white juries and bi-racial juries made similar decisions with respect to race of victims? Would that not undermine the argument of McCleskey?

It seems to me that good social science would demand that the dispositions of black *vs.* white decision-makers be compared before jumping to the conclusion that decisions by whites are critically different from decisions by blacks. For example, there are a number of studies that look at decisions by black *vs.* white police officers, prison guards and judges and most have not found that race of decision-maker was significant. Surely the Supreme Court should not overturn the death penalty on the unproven assumption that the decisions by white *vs.* black prosecutors and jurors are substantially different. Again, the Baldus study did not even establish the race of the decision-makers — and it certainly did not establish that white prosecutors and jurors differed in their decisions from black prosecutors and jurors!

What good would it do to compare decisions by white *vs.* black decision-makers? Baldus claims that he controlled for all critical variables and that a 4.3:1 disparity by race of victim remained. Thus he infers that race of victim must explain the 4.3:1 disparity. My point is that the negative inference (of racism) would not be made if decision-makers were black as well as white. Suppose that the same disparity existed in decisions made by all-white and bi-racial juries. It would then be difficult to claim that black jurors, like white jurors, exercised a subtle racial bias against those who killed white victims.

And if the statistics still indicated a disparity by race of victim, even when race of decision-maker was considered, one might consider some non-racial factors that might be correlated with race of victim. For example, it is likely that social class of victim is an important factor in seeking the death penalty in that the office of the prosecutor feels more pressured (via phone calls, pressure groups like Parents of Murdered Children) when more 'prominent' people are killed. This factor alone might explain why black on white killings seem to receive more severe treatment than black on black killings. It would appear that many killings of whites involve middle and upper-class victims while most killings of blacks involve offenders and victims of the lower class. Thus what appears to be race of victim bias may actually be a class bias. This is not to justify greater consideration by prosecutors to victims of high social classes. It is only to suggest that what might appear to be a race of victim factor in decision-making, might actually be a class of victim factor. Baldus did not exclude this possibility (likelihood?) since he did not control for social class of victim.

FIFTH, the failure of Baldus to include controls for race of decision-maker and social class of victim and his failure to even mention the possible importance of such factors raises another important point that should be considered by any court — the possible bias of the researcher. Researchers are as subject to bias as are Supreme Court justice, prosecutors or jurors. But whereas judges and jurors are supposed to be 'neutral' prosecutors and defense attorneys, along with the statisticians on *their side*, are part of the adversary system and thus tend to present 'one-sided' views of the evidence. Since the Baldus study was intended for presentation by McCleskey, it is possible that the evidence was 'slanted'. In fact, isn't that the purpose of the adversary system?

I am not suggesting that researchers like Baldus purposely falsify their data. But the possibility remains that researchers who are advocates of a particular position (e.g., for or against the death penalty) might slant the evidence to better support the abolitionist cause. As noted above it would not help 'the cause' to mention the failure to measure race of decision-maker or social class of victim — it is better to suggest that the only inference to be drawn from the data is that of racism. There are many ways that researchers can slant or bias a study to make a stronger case for a particular position.

I am not suggesting that this bias is always conscious. Perhaps it is 'subtle'. Remember that Baldus and others have suggested that the racial bias of prosecutors and jurors is likely 'subtle' rather than conscious and direct. If prosecutors and jurors can exercise a subtle bias in their decisions why cannot researchers exercise a similar subtle bias in the design, implementation and interpretation of their studies? Surely it is hypocritical to suggest that researchers are free from bias while prosecutors and jurors — and Supreme Court Justices — are not.

Perhaps the adversary system is a poor forum for the presentation of statistical data. If so, 'truth' might be better served if the Supreme Court turned over all of the data to some body such as the National Academy of Sciences, and asked both sides to make their case to that body. The Academy could then give its opinion on the validity of the statistics and the conclusions of the researchers to the Court. Surely the Academy is more qualified and less biased (since they are less likely to be as emotionally involved in the issue) than the researchers or the Court? But that will never happen because the Court (and researchers) will never admit that its bias influences its decisions.

The perception of bias is also one-sided when one considers the impact of bias on the part of the Supreme Court Justices. I believe that the Court majority decided to uphold the death penalty and then marshaled its evidence and logic in support of that decision. Critics of the death penalty will agree. But I also believe that the dissenting Justices decided to rule for McCleskey and that this decision influenced their view of the validity of the Baldus study. I doubt if death penalty critics will agree with that assessment. But why is it that 'they' (supporters of the death penalty, including the Court majority) are biased while 'we' (critics of the death penalty, including the dissenting Justices) are not? In my view, prejudice is the attribution of negative traits and motives to 'them' and positive traits and motives to 'us'.

I wonder what abolitionists would say if a study funded by the National District Attorney's Association (NDAA) found no evidence of racial bias in the death penalty. Surely, it would be argued that the study was possibly influenced by bias. It should be noted that the Baldus study was funded in part by the Legal Defense Fund of the NAACP. Did that support influence the research? If not, why would one doubt a study funded by the NDAA.

A few years ago both the International Association of Chiefs of Police (IACP) and the National Urban League sponsored research to determine if there was a racial bias in the use of deadly force by the police. The IACP found no such bias while the Urban League reported the opposite conclusion. Does anyone doubt that *both* were biased?

I am an ardent advocate of gun control and I know that there is a strong temptation to 'slant' my research to support my position. I have no doubt that a similar bias is evident in research supported by the National Rifle Association. I have noted that most of the researchers who are involved in death penalty research are abolitionists, some being so ardent in their support of this cause that they appear publicly to denounce the death penalty. Are we supposed to believe that this advocacy does not influence their research? I am the first to admit that my position on gun control, the death penalty, etc., does influence my research.

I get the distinct impression from critics of the McCleskey decision that they believe all 'competent' social scientists agree that the Baldus study has resolved the 'race effect' issue. But I am not convinced when the McCleskey defense team selects one or more prominent social scientists to tell the Supreme Court that everyone agrees with the methods and conclusions of Baldus. (It should be noted that competent statisticians testified for the State of Georgia that the Baldus study was not valid). If that is the case, why isn't this issue turned over to a more neutral body of social scientists? Many prominent social scientists do not agree that the Baldus study proves what it purports to prove. Certainly I do not believe that. My view is that the issue of racial bias by race of victim in the death penalty is unresolved.

SIXTH, one test of a research methodology is to see if it would be accepted by its advocates if applied to a different issue where the ensuing 'proof' would go against the bias of the researcher. The Baldus methodology involved the use of regression analysis to control for various factors to determine if the 11:1 race of victim disparity in the Georgia death penalty could be accounted for by such legitimate considerations as type of homicide, aggravation level, whether torture was used, and so forth. After a number of these variables were utilized as controls, a 4.3:1 disparity remained (though this disparity was not statistically significant) and that remaining disparity was viewed as a race effect. However, many statisticians would call the remaining variation after controls the 'unexplained' variation — though it might include a true race effect.

Suppose one used the type of regression analysis utilized by Baldus to explain the disparity in grading in classes taught by the Baldus research team and found that black students (or males, etc.) received lower grades than white students. Does anyone believe that the team would agree that racism was present in *their* grading? I would imagine that they would argue that the 'model did not fit the decision process' or that 'important control variables were not utilized' (these arguments have been raised by critics of the Baldus death penalty study).

It is also interesting to note that the black/white disparity (20:1) in the National Basketball Association (NBA) is greater than the black/white disparity by race of victim in the Georgia death penalty (11:1). Suppose I used the same type of analysis as that used by Baldus and found that a 4.3:1 disparity still remained (after controlling for such factors as vertical leap, points per games, rebounds, assists, etc.). Would the remaining disparity (4.3:1) be the 'race factor' indicating that whites were being discriminated against? Or perhaps we could infer 'racial superiority' (for blacks) from this data? If intent can be inferred from statistical disparity it appears that one could 'prove' any theory (e.g., type of intent or 'cause') from the disparity in outcome that remains after controls (e.g., allegedly after 'all other things are equal').

The remaining disparity may be due to factors not measured and controlled (e.g., interest in the game, other career opportunities, quickness, 'heart', etc.); to the failure of the statistical model to simulate the decision process; to a race factor; or to a combination of these factors. Baldus only accounted for 50% of the variance in his model, indicating either that many important decision factors were not included or that the mind of criminal justice officials does not work in the simple fashion utilized in the statistical model.

And why is it that when studies reach a conclusion favored by abolitionists (e.g., like the study by William Bowers that found a 'brutalization effect' rather than a deterrent effect for the death penalty), one listens in vain for criticisms of the methodology? Was Bowers' methodology really that much more valid than that of Isaac Ehrlich (who said that each execution deters 8 murders) or was the criticism directed against the methodology of Ehrlich (but not Bowers) based on a disagreement with his conclusions? After all, why criticize 'our side' when it might hurt 'the cause'. Abolitionists criticize the logic of the U.S. Supreme Court in McCleskey because the Court came to the 'wrong' conclusion. But when the Massachusetts Supreme Court invalidated that state's death penalty based on data suggesting racial discrimination in *other states* (no one was even on death row in Massachusetts at the time), abolitionists did not criticize the court's logic since the Court came to the 'right' decision.

SEVENTH, McCleskey would have the U.S. Supreme Court adopt a theory of racial discrimination that is inferred from the remaining variation after controls — one that is quite vague. Just how does race of victim enter into the consciousness (or unconsciousness) of prosecutors and juries, especially when race of defendant appears to have little or no impact. It would seem that those who propose such a theory should spell out the mechanisms in some detail and account for the 'facts' that are known.

Perhaps the most elaborate attempt to describe the actual psychological mechanism is that by Gross and Mauro. After describing the cursory prior attempts at developing a 'discrimination theory', Gross and Mauro set forth an explanation that attempts to account for the fact that race of defendant appears not to be a factor in jury decision-making while race of victim does. They hypothesize that white jurors are aware of the possible biasing effect of race of defendant and thus attempt to counteract that bias. However, the race of victim operates more subtly on the voting (for life or death) of jurors. We are told that white jurors, not being alert to the dangers of bias by race of victim, may empathize or identify more with white victims and thus be more horrified by the murder of whites, thus seeing those cases as more deserving of the death penalty.

No evidence is presented to substantiate this theory of racial discrimination. The obvious solution, if the theory is valid, is for the court to alert white jurors to the danger of race of victim bias so they can consciously counteract that subtle bias as they do for the more direct bias that may occur by race of defendant.

Any theory set forth has to explain why race of defendant does not appear to impact on white jurors while race of victim does. But if racism is as pervasive as McCleskey argues, how can it be so easily overcome with respect to race of defendant. And if the counteracting can be accomplished by an act of will, why can't that same will overcome the bias by race of victim? If the Gross and Mauro theory is correct, we do not need to abolish the death penalty — we just need to issue a cautionary warning to jurors about the dangers of bias by race of victim.

Furthermore, how does this theory explain why there is no significant race of victim disparity in such states as New Jersey, Pennsylvania, North Carolina and Delaware in the imposition of the death penalty? Would McCleskey agree that since there is no race of victim disparity in these (and possibly other) states, there is no racism in the imposition of the death penalty in these states? McCleskey appears to argue that the death penalty cannot be imposed in a racist society without racial bias. But, if that is the case, how does one explain why there appears to be no racial disparity in some states by the same type of statistical evidence that is used to indicate a racial disparity in Georgia? I would predict that the response of death penalty critics would be that though there is no statistical evidence of racial bias in some states, it probably operates on a more 'subtle' level. That sounds like a non-falsifiable thesis doesn't it? If we find evidence of a race of victim disparity, that proves racism. If we find no race of victim disparity, that does not disprove racism. In fact, the latter proves that racism has only gone 'underground' and is more subtle.

I have faced this kind of argument in response to my book, *The Myth of a Racist Criminal Justice System*. When I point out that conviction rates and sentencing patterns in most studies indicate no disparity by race of defendant, I am told that racism is still there but operating subtly. Thus, if the data indicate no race disparity we are told that does not indicate an absence of racism, but if the data does indicate race disparity, that is proof of racism. Thus it would appear that statistics are a handy tool — they can help your argument but they can't hurt it.

EIGHTH, I am concerned about what I see as a type of 'moral arrogance' and 'elitism' on the part of abolitionists in viewing those who support the death penalty. One gets the strong impression that abolitionists see the public view (and those who support it) in favor of the death penalty as being on a more 'primitive' moral level. Surely there is room for debate on the issue of the morality of the death penalty? Why do those who poke fun at the moral absolutism of a Jerry Falwell take the view that abolitionists are on a higher moral plane in refusing to give in to the bloodthirsty masses? Where is the 'natural law' or God-given code that forbids the death penalty?

Abolitionists say they are as concerned about the victim of murder as anyone else, but do not believe that executions achieve a useful purpose. But if that is the case, why are Abolitionists generally present at candlelight vigils at executions but rarely at candlelight vigils to commemorate the victims of killers? It is bad enough that the families of murder victims have to endure a lifetime of grief. But it is deeply insulting to them to be portrayed as 'moral primitives' by those posing as the 'moral elite'. I fail to see how a higher morality is evidenced by those who plead for mercy for killers rather than by those who plead for justice for the families of victims.

CHAPTER 12

Repressive Formalism

Dragan Milovanovic
Northeastern Illinois University

The 'no discrimination thesis' (NDT) has been argued on many levels. Although much empirical analysis and critique indicates that many methodological problematics exist and that hot debates and polemics will continue, initiated most recently, by Wilbanks' book *The Myth of a Racist Criminal Justice System*, I would like to shift to an additional dimension in this debate, that of the policy implications of the NDT. The debate fueled by Wilbanks' thesis, I think, is quite productive. Arguments by fiat, broad proclamations of truth, or by assertion without substantiation is idle chatter for both the Right or the Left. Not attending to Wilbanks' often poignant and controversial statistical analysis is tantamount to an abdication to the momentum generated by the Right (For a general critique of the often underlying 'us versus them' attitude see, Lynch, 1989; Groves, 1989). In fact, recent court decisions have increasingly turned to (be it rather unwillingly) statistical evidence in their rulings. Here I want to briefly comment on the U.S. Supreme Court decision, *McCleskey* v. *Kemp* (1987), which can be seen as one of the clearest examples of the Court imposing legalistic reasoning in race discrimination cases over social scientific reasoning, and on two 'reverse discrimination' cases. In each case, I will argue, the search for a conspiratorial, instrumental marxist explanation is unsatisfactory; rather, the Courts find themselves in a pragmatic situation demanding the perpetuation of myths or cloaks in maintaining homeostasis in the social formation. In response to the various legitimation crises the Courts come through with their verbalizations that are quite compatible with maintaining the status quo, and in that sense, are in fact tools for the maintenance of discrimination and other forms of oppression in our society.

Freeman's analysis (1982) of antidiscrimination law in general is well taken. He indicates that the Courts have gradually moved away from a 'conditions' examination — lack of jobs and political power, brutalizing work places, segregated schools, etc. — to a 'type-of-person' examination in causes of discrimination. And whereas the courts beginning with *Brown* v. *Board of Education* (1954) were more concerned with the former, since

An earlier version of this essay, entitled "Repressive Formalism: Perpetuating Discrimination Through 'Benevolent' Anti-Discrimination Law", appeared in The Humanist Sociologist Spring, 1988, Vol 13, No 2.

1974, they have moved to the latter focus as explanations for racism in our society. Coupled with the Court's stipulation that mere statistical evidence of race or gender disparities is not constitutive of 'proof' and that "intent to discriminate' must also be proven, the Courts have effectively removed themselves from progressive policy questions, deferring to system sustaining rationales. And even where the Courts focus on formalistic reasoning what remains hidden are substantive issues.

Wilbanks' analysis of *McCleskey* v. *Kemp* in the attendant essay in this book is quite correct on many points but rather shy in its analysis of the their ramifications particularly as to policy. I would certainly agree with Wilbanks: that the Court did 'cop-out', particularly as to the question of statistical 'evidence'; that it did have its conclusions in advance and then developed its rationale later; that its stipulated required burden of 'direct discriminatory intent' is practically impossible to meet; that the Court was scared off by the thought that future social scientists would present contradictory 'evidence' and create uncertainty in court decisions; that the Baldus statistical study (1983) indicating a 4.3:1 race disparity in the imposition of the death penalty, after controlling for over 200 variables, critically missed the critical control variable of 'class' and even if it did not, did not control for decision-makers' (prosecutors' and jurors') race and gender. In fact, Wilbanks quite convincingly argues that class effects were confounded with race effects and that perhaps it was the former that was of greater weight as a predictor variable. But Wilbanks' examination does not then go on to reflect on the ramifications. Clearly, critical criminologists would want to address the wider question of the *conditions* producing statistical disparities, even, for the sake of argument, accepting Wilbanks' contention that there is no race discrimination in decision making in the criminal justice system. Therefore two clear spheres can be discernable: political economic configurations and judicial processing. System generated hierarchical practices at the former level could be quite effectively hidden at the latter level by formalistic legal discourse, presumably centered on 'free choice' of agents in the social formation on the one hand (and hence blaming the victim), or on malicious agents ('bad apples') on the other. Thus we could reason at a formalistic level (legalistic) and show that equally situated were equally treated only by making the equivalence equation restricted to certain variables (i.e., devoid of political economic factors). In other words, substantive questions can be conveniently omitted by the definitional constraints within equal protection analysis done by the courts (= repressive formalism). Here, the political question was conveniently avoided by the courts as was also the case in the two 'reverse discrimination' cases discussed below.

What was notably unusual about the Georgia case was that the District, Appeals, and the U.S. Supreme Court found themselves within two distinct discourses — legalistic and scientific — in order to resolve the question of race effects in the imposition of the death penalty. The justices found themselves speaking the language of statisticians — regression effects, control variables, significant tests, explained variance, etc. — and only careful legalistic gymnastics allowed them to escape and retreat to the legalistic discourse in order to stipulate that statistical proof was merely 'circumstantial evidence' (that is it is not 'direct evidence'), and that 'discriminatory purpose' must be shown, not just aggregated data pointing out statistical disparities even of a highly significant nature. Although, interestingly, the courts did indicate that "under certain limited circumstances...statistics alone [can] establish intentional discrimination" (See, *McLeskey* v. *Kemp*, 753 F.2d 877, 888 [1985]). The courts chose to have it both ways while appearing to follow precedent.

Four suggestions by Wilbanks deserve attention. First, that the Baldus study relied on by the three courts accounted for only 50% of the variance leaving the question of other important variables unexamined (i.e., the mind set of the criminal justice official, class effects, confounded class-gender-race effects, etc.). This underscores the more complex operational mode of those who would otherwise be defined as 'lackeys' of the system (often an attribution of simplistic instrumental marxist arguments). Second, Wilbanks suggests that a more prudent path the Court should have taken was perhaps to turn over the Baldus data to a body such as the National Academy of Science for resolution (both sides could argue their case and a decision could be reached that the court could then consider). Of course this overlooks the ideological dimension, a point Wilbanks seems to have forgotten when he makes a similar case with the funding of a study by the National District Attorney's Association versus the Legal Defense Fund of the NAACP. Certainly political questions would emerge and the whole process would then be open to critique. Third, Wilbanks, perhaps inadvertently, highlights the paucity of theoretically grounded empirical analyses (i.e., they are more often devoid of an underlining social theory that guides empirical examination). Here, the critical criminologist's agenda has been quite well stated by Lynch (1989: 6): critical theorists must "investigate how data can be used to assess critical theory, and it may even require that we invent new methods of analysis consistent with the critical view." I would go so far as to say that traditional positivism, a model still employed by critical/radical scholars is probably inherently anti-thetical to a dialectical approach.

Consider, for example, the undialectical nature of operationalizing variables that decontextualizes, sterilizes and produces a static conception of the social formation. Along the same lines, consider also the 'equivalence form' rooted in commodity fetishism that guides empirical investigation as it does legalistic reasoning (i.e., those based on the 'equal protection clause' of the Fourteenth Amendment to the U.S. Constitution). And fourth, consider some of the implications of Wilbanks' poignant polemics. His point is that often we use a double standard in investigating phenomena. Consider, for example, the often verbalized attacks on the 'system' for exploiting the working classes and hence the understandability of the effects of brutalization. By the same logic, can not we make a similar argument that the so called 'lackeys' of the system (police, lawyers, judges, guards, etc.) find themselves in hierarchical 'systems' that brutalize and hence their actions are 'excusable' or at least 'understandable?' Consider my review article on Ivory Tower (Milovanovic, 1990). Highly trained academics with Ph.Ds in hand often find themselves in the pragmatics of place (i.e., re-appointment, promotion, course-scheduling, sabbatical, and tenure decisions) and often fall prey to the Clark-Kent syndrome, often, in the process selling out their principles and convictions while, simultaneously, condemning the poor, uneducated, or marginalized for their inability to transcend their immediate circumstances.

To turn to two 'reverse discrimination' cases. Few things polarize the American public quicker than the notion of 'reverse discrimination.' There are those who see it as inherently evil and standing against the virtues (?) of the capitalist ethic. And then there are those who see it as a temporary, remedial step tolerable in eradicating discrimination. The polarity itself, however, is a false dichotomy. The intellectual terrain is narrow and can only lead to superficial answers to complex problems stemming from political economic imperatives. In this short space remaining I want to briefly summarize the two major Supreme Court decisions concerning 'reverse discrimination' and then argue that the results of each lead to the legal maintenance of discrimination.

Steelworkers v. *Weber* 443 U.S. 193 (1979) dealt with a private, voluntary plan established (through collective bargaining) to correct for under-representation of black workers in fifteen Kaiser Aluminum plants. Up to 1974 the plant hired craft workers who had prior skill experience. Conceded was the fact that black workers had been excluded from craft unions and thus were unable to get credentials. In 1974, 1.83% (5/273) of skilled craftworkers in the firm were black, even though the general work force in the area was 39% black. A new training program was established, with selection based on seniority with the proviso that 50% of new trainees would be black until the percentage of black skilled workers in the plant was equivalent to the percentage of blacks in the area labor market. In the first year, 13 trainees were selected, 7 of whom were black and 6 white. The most senior black trainee selected had less seniority than several white workers rejected for the program. One of the white workers rejected filed a class action suit.

The issue dealt with the Civil Rights Act of 1964, particularly section 703 (a) and (d) which together make it unlawful to "discriminate ...because of ...race." Brennan, writing the majority opinion (5-2) for the Supreme Court, concluded that no 'reverse discrimination' had taken place. The Legal Realists of the 1920s and 1930s would have been proud of the logic offered by the majority. A literal construction of 703 (a) and (d), they argued, was misplaced. Reviewing the legislative history behind the passage of the Civil Rights Act, they concluded that a strict reading of the Civil Rights Act would deny the *intent* of the legislation to eradicate existing pervasive discrimination. In support of their interpretation, the majority cited a previous case that stated "a thing may be within the letter of the statute and yet not within the statute, because not within its spirit, nor within the intention of its makers" (*Holy Trinity Church v. U.S.*, 143 U.S. 457, 1892). Conceding that the letter of the law would make the plan above unconstitutional, the majority claimed, rather, it was the 'spirit' of the law that was guiding. Thus the plan established through collective bargaining was held to be Constitutional. The criteria established in determining whether a practice constituted reverse discrimination or not included four elements: (1) that a 'manifest imbalance' (i.e., racial segregation) exists and is being corrected, (2) that white workers would not be discharged by black hirees, (3) that white workers would not be absolutely blocked from advancement, and (4) that the plan was temporary.

In *Johnson* v. *Transportation Agency* 55 L.W. 4379 (1987), the majority (6-3, Brennan again delivering the opinion) returned to the *Weber* decision. Briefly, the facts were that the Santa Clara County Transportation Agency (a public agency) voluntarily adopted a plan in promotional decisions where the sex of a qualified applicant could be considered 'as one factor.' The facts of the case indicated that whereas women constituted 36.4% of the area labor force, they only composed 22.4% of agency employees. The goal of the plan was to correct for these statistical disparities. The long range goal was to attain 36% female workers in different job titles. No specific numerical goals in the short run were set aside. The specific position in contention was a road dispatcher. Seven qualified applicants were interviewed. Johnson, a male, received a 75 in the scoring; Joyce, a female, a 73. After input by the firm's Affirmative Action Officer, Joyce was hired over Johnson. Johnson filed suit citing the Civil Right

Act as being applicable. The Supreme Court, at the outset, said *Weber* was guiding. The majority noted (and this now becomes case law) that no showing of prior discriminatory practices has to be established, but only the existence of a 'conspicuous imbalance' (i.e., statistically significant differences). In determining this imbalance, the Court argued, one must look at the percentage of minorities in the firm's work force and compare it with the percentage in the area labor market (jobs that require no 'special skills'). Where 'specialized' skills are concerned the comparison should be with those in the labor force who posses the relevant skills. Applying *Weber's* standard, the majority found that no reverse discrimination had occurred. The plan was Constitutionally acceptable.

The two cases together lay down case law. If a firm employs 98% male (or white) and 2% female (or black) workers and the area labor force is 65% male (or white) and 35% female (or black) workers in a job category that requires no special skills, then a plan introduced to try and equalize the firm's work force (consistent with the four criteria of *Weber*) could not be attacked for being discriminatory (that is, does not constitute reverse discrimination). But, if in the outside area work force 98% of the *skilled* work force was male (or white) and only 2% was female (or black), even though the area labor force as a whole was say 65% male (or white) and 35% female (or black), then no affirmative action plan would pass a Constitutional test (the permutations notwithstanding). And here lies the problem.

The courts say nothing about *conditions* themselves that provide support for the acquisition and development of skills. Clearly, inadequate educational opportunities, housing, employment opportunities, pay scales, health facilities and so forth militate against the acquisition of higher skills. A person is hard pressed to remain in a classroom on an empty stomach, with unpaid bills, no job, no adequate health services, and residing in a run down, cockroach-infested, unsafe tenement. The courts have simply avoided the issue. On the surface of the decision it seems that the problem has been liberally taken care of. And, in fact, some remediation has taken place. A socially tolerable mid-point in the polarized view toward reverse discrimination has been established. It disguises, however, fundamental economic factors that produce gross disparities in the first instance. Formalism in law legitimizes substantive injustices.

One wonders how far this decision will go. A minority member attempting to get into law or medical school or a training program, for example, who does not have the appropriate skills that other non-minority member have, could be Constitutionally denied entrance. All this is pure hyperbole. The point is that the opportunity to procure formal credentials can be traced back to fundamental socio-economic relations in society and the existence of differential life-chances that are class specific. The Courts, in their infinite wisdom, legitimize economic inequality while appearing to correct the problem. At the other end of this time frame, the higher court has already established in case law that the 'last hired first fired rule' has precedents over affirmative action programs. This effectively eviscerates any gains by minorities. If for no other reason than the increased insecurity at the work place that has been engendered for black, or female workers. This could easily be translated, psychologically, into submissive behavior.

Legal formalism, or more appropriately, repressive formalism, then, serves several purposes, or if you prefer, functions. First, it sends out an ideological message that the courts are not instruments of capitalists' interests. Real problems are perceived as being ameliorated by an independently minded judiciary. Second, the courts are seen as working within the rule of law to correct evils (even in their conjuring up metaphysical rationales like the 'spirit' of the law). Third, those most repressed in society are given evidence that they have ample opportunities. *Parens Patriae* appears in different clothing. And those most oppressed are led to believe that the legal sphere and the capitalist market place themselves are not repressive. Fourth, and following the third point closely, those who do not catch the train — the Great American Dream — have only themselves to blame (the omnipresent spectre, the 'blame-the-victim' ideology is given more fuel, nay, is given concrete expression). Fifth, divisive forces are being established and sustained between oppressed groups. Movement toward a class-for-itself is being undermined. The law in its majesty both divides and unites under the banner of law.

What is to be understood? We, as humanists and critical/radical criminologists, should temper our celebrations of small successes. No doubt some improvements do take place through anti-discrimination law. Crumbs thrown to the masses surely will allow some survival and even some assurance that things are getting better. But we should be cognizant of the hegemonic abilities, the cooptive powers and the cooling-out mechanisms of forces of domination and repression. Too, we should be aware of the continued myth-creation of the courts that legitimize hierarchical powers that are pervasive. The Court decisions in *Kemp*, *Weber*, and *Transportation Agency* indicate that the dominant political economic order will be provided with legitimization principles by legalistic discourse which is inherently shaped and sustained by capital logic, mitigated by contradictions and struggle.

REFERENCES

Baldus, D., C. Pulaski and G. Woodworth (1983), "Comparative Review of Death Sentences: An Empirical Study of the Georgia Experience" *Journal of Criminal Law and Criminology* 74(3): 661-753.

Freeman, A. (1982), "Antidiscrimination Law: A Critical Review" D. Kairys (ed.) *The Politics of Law* New York: Pantheon Books.

Groves, C. (1989), "Us and Them: Reflections on the Dialectics of Moral Hate" *The Critical Criminologist* 1(2): 3.

Lynch, Michael (1989), "Critical Theory and Quantitative Analysis: Us and Them" *The Critical Criminologist* 1(3): 6.

Milovanovic, Dragan (1990), "Ivory Tower and the Greening of a College Professor: A Review Essay of Howard Wolf's The Education of a Teacher" *Humanity and Society* 14(2): 174-191.

SECTION III:

SYNTHESIS

What Really Lies Behind The Myth of 'No Discrimination' in The Criminal Justice System

Bernard D. Headley
Northeastern Illinois University

When the editors of this volume asked me to write a reflective 'synthesis' of the articles in this volume and their overall theme, I initially hesitated — not because I was "pressed for time" or had any of the other busywork lame excuses that people in our 'profession' are so capable of manufacturing. Firstly, I had to fight off a somewhat impish urge to watch from the sidelines, because often on debates about race — to borrow from that immortal sage, Yogi Berra: "You can observe a lot by just watching." However, there was also an ambivalence stemming from a more complex, penetrating moral and philosophical struggle. I was tormented by a soul-searching question that, put in its most direct terms, asked: "Should I expend valuable energy and the scarce resource of time to direct additional attention to the outrageous ?"

Let me hasten to add that in no way was my hesitancy meant to detract from the profound respect and high esteem I hold for friends and colleagues who have chosen to challenge apologists like Professor Wilbanks, whose 'end of racism' *weltanschauung* is really an intermediate stage within a more troubling agenda. Indeed, Daniel Abeyie and Coramae Mann have presented here, once again, brilliantly crafted, well-reasoned theoretical and *qualitative* arguments as to why we should not be led into believing that racism is dead in the administration and delivery of justice in America. Zaid Ansari, E. Britt Patterson and Michael Lynch, among others, are equally impressive in their use of sophisticated *quantitative* methods in their critiques of Wilbanks in which they performed for all of us a valuable, necessary 'service'. Still, like Frederick Nietzsche, I cannot help believing that "there is a danger that when you do battle with a monster" you are likely to get soiled.

Perhaps, I am taking this all too seriously; maybe this whole polemic of whether or not there is racism in the criminal justice system falls within the realm of the prototypical academic debate — the sort of thing in which intellectuals love to engage for its own sake, *pour passer le temps*, and where, as it has been so felicitously put by Montaigne: "All I say is by way of discourse, and nothing by way of advice. I should not speak so boldly if it were my due to be believed." But having slipped quietly and unobtrusively into the back seats of crowded criminal justice conferences and various public issues fora, where I was able to observe firsthand the ferociousness with which Wilbanks and his main intellectual guru, James Q. Wilson, have defended *the* justice in the American criminal justice system — that it is doing its job, and doing it well (or, at most, that it needs to do 'more of the same') — I am convinced that this is no idle academic matter. It is deadly serious business.

Perhaps if the Wilson-Wilbanks-inspired 'no discrimination thesis' had indeed remained behind the gilded, ivyed walls of academia, I would have felt no guilt pang in watching the debate from behind the sidelines. Now, however, the issue has become a focal point of much congressional wrangling, where it is difficult to decipher whether legislators are saying there is *no* racial discrimination in the justice system; or, if there is, "so what?" A good example can be found in a recent Senate debate over a package of anti-crime measures in which righteously indignant senators fulminated over a 'racial justice' clause. The clause, proposed by Senator Edward Kennedy of Massachusetts, would have banned the death penalty in cases where racial discrimination played a part in its imposition. In a rather convoluted speech attacking the proposal, Republican, Senator Gordon Humphrey, of New Hampshire retorted: "If this race-based sentencing section is retained, Congress will effectively abolish the death penalty in those thirty-six states which have chosen to adopt capital punishment as part of their criminal justice system." The senator had inadvertently conceded the point — the painfully obvious fact that, in America, race cannot be separated from the death sentence. Disgraceful to think that he is actually *disagreeing* with Wilbanks! Democrat Bob Graham of Florida maintained that, "No jurisdiction can meet the standards of this proposal. No jurisdiction *should attempt* to meet the standards because to do so would require a fundamental shift" in the way we do justice in this country. The proposal was defeated by a vote of 58 to 38.

Whether sitting in the comfortable surroundings of the Chicago Mariott hotel at an American Society of Criminology meeting listening to the bombast of William Wilbanks, or in the cloistered setting of a college auditorium hearing out James Q. Wilson, or in the sanctuary of one's apartment watching (from the comforting distance provided by television) the rantings of unintelligible right-wing lawmakers, it is not difficult for me, a black man in America and father of two teen-age African American sons, to imagine what astute Jews in 1930s' Germany must have thought as they saw the storm clouds gathering: It's time to pack up your loved ones and move to a 'safe' country.

There is something incredulously insidious about arguing the absence of racism in any of the dominant institutions that comprise American society. All of the basic ingredients that structure one's life-chances in this country — what kind of education you receive, how far you get in school, whether you get to write books about race, where you live, where you work, how much money you make, what kind of health and medical care you receive, whether in fact you *live* or *die* — are, like it or not, determined by race. When in order to change these given racial realities — so that, in effect, one can be protected from rednecks, political demagogues, stiff-arming cops, despotic bosses, or racist bullyboys in the streets of New York — special "affirmative action" and civil rights laws have to be passed, amended, and regularly updated, it is a cruel joke to talk about the absence of racism, in whole or in part, in America.

The criminal justice system *is* America. It includes more than simply post-arrest processing. As any Introduction to Criminal Justice student should know, the system comprises a complex network of sub-institutions and the values that go with them. In fact, as Dragan Milovanovic convincingly argues, it also comprises a system of signs, language, and symbols. At any given historical moment, then, the justice system is as much a summation of America as are its television programs. If racism still permeates the entire social order — in its "education, politics, religion, and economic structure," as Coramae Mann puts it — how, pray tell, can the justice system, which is inextricably tied to nearly all of the other systems, be any *less* racist?

Arguing the absence of racism in the criminal justice system is tantamount to arguing that the whole pond may be infested, but the fish that live therein are healthy. This conception returns me to my fundamental ambivalence at being part of this entire debate. Proposing the nonexistence of racism in the criminal justice system is intended, at least so it seems to me, to goad us into a distracting sideshow, to divert our attention from the larger social reality which produces the human wreckage, "the drainage of the great festering ulcer of society,' to quote Upton Sinclair, in which the justice system serves as custodian. So getting into a fit over the presence or absence of racism in the American criminal justice system is really like worrying about the style of your haircut "when you're about to be beheaded", as put so aptly by Professor Harry Edwards.

Using federal government data, the Sentencing Project, in Washington, D.C., tells us that on any given day in 1989: "Almost one in four (23 percent) Black men in the age group 20-29 [were] either in prison, jail, on probation, or parole..."; 610,000 African American men in the same 20-29 age group were under the control of the justice system, while only 436,000 African American men *of all ages* were in college; an African American male is six times more likely to go to prison than his white counterpart; and one out of four African American men *will* go to prison in his lifetime (*i.e.*, excluding jail or being placed on probation, etc.). Moreover, as Michael Albert, writing in the April 1990 issue of **Z**, tells us: "We have gotten to the point where the survival prospects of an average young Black person in a major city in 1990 are not much better than those of young Black Panthers at the height of the police repression...in the late 1960s."

Maybe I just don't get it, but is this not saying something about a trend, about a systematic pattern, about a correlation between race and a certain outcome in the criminal justice system?

But, aha! There I go using that dirty little word, 'outcome'. The issue, Wilbanks tells us, is not whether there are certain peculiar racial 'outcomes' in criminal justice processing; it is whether racism (or discrimination) was 'intended'. If intention cannot be proved as existing inside the head of police officers, prosecutors, defense attorneys, judges, jurors, caseworkers, probation and correction officers, then it is ridiculous to talk about racism. Leaving aside the fact that Wilbanks misses (perhaps *intentionally* ?) the whole point of institutionalized racism, using his logic, we could argue that the slave system was not really racist, since the basic 'intent' of the slavemasters was to improve profitability, not to discriminate against Africans — a point made by the economic historian Eric Williams. White capital was not particularly 'hung up' on which racial or ethnic group it exploited, Williams contends. "It would have gone to the moon for labor, if necessary." Were the slavemasters then non-discriminators because they were driven more by economic motives than a desire to subjugate a particular racial group? The answer is really quite moot. The judgment of history is of the entire *slave system* — of its processes and institutionalized order. The commonly agreed upon position that slavery was a racist abomination is not based on a determination of what was in the heads of specific slavemasters, or on some unknown (and unknowable) notion of 'intent'. Rather, it is a judgment made on the basis of a visible, manifest *outcome*.

For what other reason are there civil rights laws, open-housing statutes, and court-mandated bussing — except to address certain embarrassing racial outcomes? My suspicion that the Wilbanks crowd is more than aware of all of this, begs the question: what really lies behind their 'no discrimination' smokescreen ?

The real 'intent' of this death-of-racism argument is given away when Wilbanks suggests that, "if anything", the criminal justice system often bends over backwards to be lenient to blacks. In other words, the justice system, like so many other institutions (public and private) in the post-civil rights era, is guilty of racial excess, to the point where it now engages in "reverse discrimination". This position is clearly in keeping with the 1980s' Reagan political-ideological *zeitgeist*, where, to quote Michael Omi and Howard Winant, "issues of race have been dramatically revived...in the form of a 'backlash' to the political gains of racial minority movements of the past. Conservative popular movements, academics and the Reagan administration joined hands [sic] to attack the legacy and logic of earlier movements", having done so in a way "which escapes obvious charges of racism."

Therefore, the 'no discrimination thesis' in the workings of the criminal justice system must be seen in the same light as the claim made by the Reagan-reconstituted U.S. Commission on Civil Rights (headed by, yes, a black man, Clarence Pendleton) that we "are working on a color blind society that has opportunities for all and guarantees success for none." For the Reagan-Bush crowd, unless 'intent' could be 'proved', it was silly to talk about redress of discriminatory practices. As a matter of fact, if there was any discrimination at all, it was *against* white men. Thus we should expect, that in *The Myth of a Racist Criminal Justice System Part II*, an even more forceful argument will be made, using — what else? — 'hard, empirical data' to show that the justice system is not only sending *less* African Americans to prison than it ought to, but that it treats white males unfairly. Wan'na bet?

REFERENCES

Albert,M. (1990) "Amandla" *Z Magazine*, April:67.

Mauer, M. (1990) *Young Black Men and The Criminal Justice System: A Growing National Problem,* Washington, D.C.: The Sentencing Project.

Omni, M. and H. Winant (1986) *Racial Formation in The United States*, New York: RKP.

Whitman, S. (1988) *Can't Jail The Spirit: Political Prisoners in The U.S.*, Claremont, Il.: El Coqui.

Williams, E. (1944) *Capitalism and Slavery*, New York: Putman.

Wilson, J. Q. and R. J. Herrnstein (1985) *Crime and Human Nature*, New York: Simon and Schuster

CHAPTER 14

Boundary Maintenance and Discrimination in Canadian and U.S. Society

Laurence French
Western New Mexico University

As a synthesizer, I will attempt to react to the various arguments from the majority/minority boundary maintenance perspective. In doing so, the empirical (so called 'objective') orientation is viewed within the scope of the philosophy of science. The central theme here is that all societies are biased and that these biases are reflected in their respective epistemological methodologies. Given this premise, societal ideals of justice are means with selective application. Moreover, societies often have a double standard regarding their judicial means — one for the accepted dominant group and yet another for those deemed unacceptable (minority groups within the society; other societies). To illustrate this point the U. S. today offers its judicial ideals to members of the dominant society (including white collar and political offenders) while at the same time subscribing to a 'radical' judicial model for societies it is interested in overthrowing. In between lies a perversion of our judicial ideals as they are applied to 'negative' minorities (ghetto Blacks and Latinos; American Indians...).

Another element of my argument is the contention that we as individuals are biased as well. Indeed, we must constantly strive for objectivity — a process complicated by limited means toward obtaining ultimate 'truths'. While science is a means toward determining truth, it is an imperfect process, and it certainly should not be viewed in a vacuum (raw empiricism) or as an end in itself. The scientific method is merely a means towards 'truth', and, therefore, can be, and easily is, culturally biased. That is the dominant (majority) cultural view generally prevails as the 'truth' — a phenomenon known as ethnocentrism.

EPISTEMOLOGY AND THE CRIMINAL JUSTICE SYSTEM

This argument about the relativistic nature of 'truth' extends to Plato's *Allegory of the Cave* in which he suggests that our view of reality is tempered through our socialization and enculturation. During the sixteenth century, Fràncis Bacon termed these biases 'idols'. Bacon's four idols are: idols of the theatre (appeal to authority), idols of the tribe (group biases), idols of the market-place (common prejudice), and idols of the cave (individual biases). The latter is an elaboration of Plato's individualized social/psychological bias we all develop as part and parcel of our personality.

Earlier this century, the work of two European social philosophers, Max Weber and Emile Durkheim, greatly influenced contemporary social scientific theory. Focusing on individual biases, Weber warned that as scientists, we are never 'ethically neutral' (totally objective). Instead, we must strive for objectivity. In doing so, we must be aware of both our 'value orientation' and our 'value reference'. The former refers to our value system (emergent biases such as professional interests), while the latter reflects family and group biases acquired through our formative socialization (class, race, education, family-orientation, religion).

On the other hand, Durkheim alerted us to the 'collective will' and 'collective realities'. Here he talked of the relationship between epistemology and social control. In this argument, socialization and public policy determine collective emotions such as prejudice and discrimination within society. The relationship between epistemological methodologies and social control is perhaps best articulated by Erich Goode:

> All civilizations set rules concerning what is real and what is not, what is true and what false. All societies select out of the data before them a world, one world, the world taken for granted, and declare that the real world. Each one of these artificially constructed worlds is to some degree idiosyncratic, unique. No individual views reality directly, in the raw, so to speak. Our perceptions are narrowly channeled through concepts and interpretations. What is commonly thought of as reality, that which exists, or simply is, is a set of suppositions, rationalizations, justifications, defenses, all generally collectively agreed-upon, which guide and channel each individual's perceptions in a specific and distinct direction. The specific rules governing the perception of the universe which man inhabits are more or less arbitrary, a matter of convention. Every society establishes a kind of espistemological methodology (1969:84).

Add to this Durkheim's contention that all societies across-cultures and across-time define certain behaviors as deviant (criminal) in order to placate the public that boundaries are being maintained, and we begin to see the roots of institutionalized (both *defacto* and *dejure*) discrimination within U. S. society today. To state that the United

States *was* a racist society is certainly an understatement. But to use the 'objective data' argument to obviate any remnants of institutional racism today is absurd. And I must agree with Coramae Mann that to proselytize this view is dangerous. Majority/minority relations rarely reach irreversible milestones. Instead, these relationships are generally more cyclic. This is evident in the rise of anti-semitism and inter-ethnic animosities throughout Europe, the Soviet Union and the Middle East.

In our own country there is increased racism on college campuses. In a June 1, 1990 release, the National Institute Against Prejudice and Violence noted that one in five minority college students is the victim of racial attacks (1 million each year), and that former President Reagan's policies are at least partly to blame. Along similar lines, Division 45 of the American Psychological Association sees the relationship of racism and public policy as a major obstacle in American society. Add to this the vigilance of minority watchdog organizations such as the United Church of Christ's Commission for Racial Justice, the Southern Prison Ministry's Southern Coalition Report on Jails and Prisons, and the Native American Rights Fund (NARF), and it becomes readily apparent that we are far from being a non-racist society with a non-discriminating criminal justice system.

So what about the argument that individuals can be prejudiced while the 'system' is not? Our 'system' has long had biases (prejudices) which manifest themselves in public policy (discrimination). Racial minorities have long been on the receiving end of this process. The concept of 'manifest destiny' allowed us to exploit Blacks, American Indians, Hispanics, and Orientals. These minorities were, and in many instances continue to be, defined as the pariahs of our society — those outside the boundaries of our judicial ideals; however, in order to justify these actions, dominant society first needs to define the parameters of exclusion. In this way, a self-fulfilling prophecy is constructed in which these 'outsiders' appear to deserve what happens to them (blaming the victim ideology).

This symbolic labeling of visible 'outsiders' as being beyond salvation has a long and persistent history with regards to American Indians. From the first European contacts until the late nineteenth century the official Colonial/U.S. policy was that of physical genocide. Since then it has been an active policy of 'cultural genocide' — a term similar to the concept of 'petit Apartheid' advanced in this book by Daniel Georges-Abeyie. This process of cultural genocide is well illustrated in the article about Mandatory Supervision in Canada and its implication for Native offenders by Walter DeKeseredy and Brian MacLean. Underlying the minority labeling process and its generation of a negative self-fulfilling prophecy (American Indian cultural genocide) is the manipulation of socio-economic and psycho-cultural factors (Federal Paternalism) so that these people fail. The desired end product is 'marginality' — a cultural form of alienation (K. Marx, S. Freud, E. Fromm) in which American Indians (or any other alienated minority group) are not adequately socialized in either their minority culture or the dominant society. Thus the failures of American Indians in Canada and the U. S. before both society and the criminal justice system is reflective of Thorsten Sellin's process of 'secondary conflict', and Eric Erickson's 'confused role identity' (identity crises). Even with these policies of accommodation (Federal Paternalism) some American Indians are assimilated into the dominant society. However, the majority who do not desire to abandon their traditional culture should not be punished for making this choice. Expanding this process to Blacks and Latinos we realize that there have always been class and color differences within the groups themselves. Nonetheless, the 'middle class' minority often carried their own negative stereotype among their own people — 'apple', 'oreo', 'Uncle Tom'.

A critical part of this argument is that even "middle class' minorities are subject to the biases of the criminal justice system. It is difficult to ignore the arguments presented in the text such as the 'Black shift phenomenon' and Mann's contention that not a single white defendant has been executed for killing a minority person since *Gregg* v. *Georgia*. It seems that things have not changed much since Garfinkel's eleven year study of the North Carolina system over fifty years ago (1949). He found that Blacks killing Blacks was okay, that Whites killing Blacks was okay, that Whites killing Whites required the fair administration of justice, but that Blacks killing Whites required blood vengeance — with or without the administration of justice. Recently, police departments in major cities have arrested young black males *en masse* as a result of public outcries relevant to the alleged attack of a white victim by a black (The Chuck Stuart case in Boston is one example).

Given these arguments it certainly seems difficult to separate common (public) prejudices from discriminatory practices within the criminal justice system — especially when the 'system' generally reflects a more conservative view of the dominant value system itself. Quinney stated this process well in his work, *Critique of Social Order*. Instead of addressing the social problems surrounding the riots of the 1960s, the Omnibus Crime Control and Safe Streets Act merely created a more forceful control mechanism, The Law Enforcement Assistance Administration (LEAA) designed to foster J. Edgar Hoover's biased criminal image — that of the minority 'street criminal'. It became an expensive experiment in 'blaming the victim' for which we are still paying. The National Advisory Commission on Higher

Education for Police Officers (1979) addressed the reinforcement process as it pertained to criminal justice education by stating that the present structure of police education often results in little more than tacking credits on to police personnel, and serving the *status quo* in policing rather than stimulating change. A number of recommendations were then offered suggesting the dismantling of academic 'cop shops' and putting an end to field-oriented staff and political cronyism. It went on to state that education background, teaching ability, research and commitment — rather than prior employment in a criminal justice agency — should be the most important criteria of faculty selection, tenure and promotion in criminal justice programs. The intention here, I presume, was to freshen up the use of epistemological methodology within criminal justice education which, in turn, greatly influences the administration of justice. I think it is safe to say that this process has not happened. Instead, we see the cronyism issue surface again with the same people and, consequently, the same self-serving perspective being involved in these 'critical' reassessments of criminal justice education.

Another discriminatory trend within U. S. society today is the movement from proactive (preventive) treatment to reactive punishment. We are dismantling our treatment facilities under the guise of 'de-institutionalization' while engaged in the rapid growth of incarceration facilities. There is little mystery as to what message the dominant society is currently sending its members. It is no wonder why the death penalty is so popular a public sentiment — especially for 'street criminals' (stereotyped minorities). Again to use the American Indian to illustrate this problem, they fear the recent attempt to expand the federal death sentence to reservations. It is known by tribal leaders as the 'American Indian Death Penalty'. And to add insult to injury, the Federal Government is doing this at a time when they are eliminating support for Indian education. This is clearly another example of planned marginality, yet this time with the focus back on physical genocide.

Part of the problem with criminal justice education and its influence on the administration of justice is the so-called empirical image of crime and criminals in U. S. society. Hoover gave us the 'Index Crimes' along with their obvious class and minority biases. They have been long used to define the boundaries of acceptability as prescribed by the dominant society. His biases gained wide acceptance within the discipline of criminal justice with the 'empirical' work of such noted criminologists as Wolfgang and Amir. I see this as the fallacy of *ex post facto* secondary analysis of data. To illustrate this phenomenon I will glean excerpts from my earlier article (French, 1979/80).

The advent of computerized statistical packages as well as the availability of computer data banks have been lauded as significant technological advances, especially for the social sciences. Interestingly, it is the near irrefutable image that scientific quantification connotes which seems to be the root cause of this dilemma. The cost and time benefits aside, computerized research has a major methodological shortcoming in that it allows for research to be elevated from its intended purpose, that of an epistemological 'means', to becoming an 'end' in itself. Thus it is not uncommon for secondary researchers to 'milk' data banks in their search for correlational or factor relationships. Often this *ex post facto* research is then used to generate articles and the dissemination of erroneous or misleading findings. Primary *ex post facto* analysis is problematic in itself mainly due to the inference factor. That is, oftentimes it is extremely difficult to determine causal factors after-the-fact (separation of error from truth). Clearly, this problem becomes compounded where secondary analysis is involved. Few secondary researchers are cognizant of the primary research design or the methods of data collection. Nonetheless, much research has been generated from these sources with many secondary researchers basing their conclusions upon the *a priori* assumption that their secondary data sources were accurate. This becomes a serious ethical issue when these data misrepresent minority criminality.

Wolfgang's (1958) homicide and Amir's (1971) rape studies are considered to be classics serving as unchallenged models of society's most serious forms of violence. Apparently, Wolfgang's study involved a secondary analysis of the Philadelphia police (Homicide Squad) files for the period January 1, 1948 to December 31, 1952. From these data he found that 621 offenders killed 588 victims, and more significant to his theoretical perspective, 26 percent (150 cases) involved victim precipitation (VP). Thus, he concluded that VP homicides are characterized by: (1) Black victims, (2) Black offenders, (3) male victims and so forth.

A decade later, Amir published his research on 'forcible rape'. Again the data involved a secondary analysis of Philadelphia's police (Morals Squad) file. Amir used data collected from January 1 to December 31 for the years 1958 and 1960. From these data (646 victims and 1,292 offenders), he established certain rape characteristics and patterns, notably that Blacks are over-represented in rape statistics, both as victims and as offenders, and that extremely violent rapes usually involve Black men and white women.

Both these studies have been widely cited in criminal justice, criminology, deviance, and social problem texts with attention usually limited to their summary characteristics and with little attention paid to the methodology or the limitations of these studies. Indeed, these studies are usually portrayed as being representative of the U. S. in general. A consequence of this dissemination of 'empirical data' has been a general misconception among college and university students, most of whom are white, across the nation and beyond. Hence Blacks are now commonly associated with criminal violence such as murder and rape. While both authors mentioned the limitations of their research, that is, the fact that it involved a particular eastern city, Philadelphia, they did not challenge the reliability of the primary data source or the racial bias of the police force (Rizzo syndrome).

THE HINDELANG/WILBANKS BIAS

The Wolfgang study is important to my discussion because it dates the Hindelang/Wilbanks' racial bias to at least 1977 and the nationwide 'Education Project in Criminal Justice' at the State University of New York at Albany (SUNY-A). Funded through the LEAA it was described as representing a comprehensive and multifaceted effort to achieve a number of important objectives in the area of minority involvement in criminal justice higher education. This was the time when SUNY-A was producing the ***LEAA Sourcebook*** under the direction of Michael Hindelang. Like myself, both Hindelang and Wilbanks were involved in the 'Minority Justice' project. The overall director was the Dean of the School of Criminal Justice at SUNY-A — the late Donald Newman.

This project was flawed from the beginning. Replete with cronyism and a authoritarian (Theory X, cop shop) organizational style, a predetermined hierarchy of faculty were selected to teach minority faculty about the minority perspective. At the top was Donald Newman and four SUNY-A faculty whose status was that of 'Full Professors'. Next were the eight designated 'teachers' and 'supervisors' who were assigned the status of 'Professor Associates'. Lastly came the twenty 'College Instructors' (regardless of their real academic rank). I was part of this last group. We supposedly were selected because of our work with minority justice. The 'College Instructors' consisted of thirteen Blacks (3 females and 10 males), and one each from the following categories: Oriental, Chicano, Cuban, Arab, southern White, French-Canadian, and a WASP.

This flawed structure, nonetheless, is credited with forcing confrontations which quickly brought out both the racial condescension of some and the outright racism of others. Hindelang, known mostly for his role as a biased 'raw empiricist', we could understand. After all here was the arch conservative graduate from the most radical criminology program (since dismantled) in the country (University of California, Berkeley). But Wilbanks posed a serious dilemma. Was this not the same Wilbanks involved in the highly acclaimed and critical report on Attica (The Official Report of the New York State Special Commission on Attica) — a report which documented institutional racism within the New York correctional system?

Yet, during the 'Minority Justice' project, there was Wilbanks, at Hindelang's knee, both aggressively supporting Wolfgang's 'empirical thesis' of greater criminality among Blacks. Similar sentiments emerge again in the Wilbanks' selections in this book. His reference to a justifiable white backlash; his pretense that his literature search and review is both comprehensive and 'objective', his criticism of his critics of not being 'objective', and his justification for increased executions based upon his apparent 'emotional' concern for the families of victims and their right for vengeance are all indicative of his biases and the illogic of his contention that the NDT is founded on a purely objective premise without any prejudicial influences.

Going back to Weber's value reference and value orientation Wilbanks, in my judgement as both a criminologist and psychologist, needs to reassess his biases and determine why he is so bent on proselytizing the NDT. Is it to carry on the Hindelang torch of discriminatory empiricism? Is it for some unfulfilled personal needs which are compensated for while on the 'talk show circuit?' At any rate, I can not help but agree with both Mann and Georges-Abeyie that the Wilbanks' crusade is on a dangerous path. The good thing is that the likely converts to a thesis such as his are those within the criminal justice system already predisposed toward an 'empirical' exoneration of their obvious prejudices. Look at how many of us who were indoctrinated with the Wolfgang racism myth yet survived its influence.

REFERENCES

Amir, M., 1971 *Patterns in Forcible Rape*, Chicago: University of Chicago Press.

French, L., (1979/1980) "The Need for Qualitative Interpretations of Criminal Justice Research: The American Minority Situation" *Crime and Justice*, 7/8:209-213.

Goode, E., (1969) "Marijuana and the Politics of Reality" *Journal of Health and Social Behavior,* vol 10 (June): 83-94.

Wolfgang, M., (1958) *Patterns in Criminal Homicide*, Philadelphia: University of Pennsylvania Press.

CHAPTER 15

Carpe Diem (Seize the Day!):
An Opportunity for Feminist Connections

Mona Danner / Jean Landis

The American University

The title of this essay reflects our belief in this collective response to the publication of Wilbanks' *The Myth of a Racist Criminal Justice System* as an act of resistance by critical criminologists. It effectively destabilizes traditional academic thought and practice, and invites criminologists to seize the day in reshaping debates bearing on the problem of racism and criminal justice "in ways that suggest new theoretical insights and empirical directions" (Thomas and O'Maolchatha 1989).

Drawing on feminist literature, in this essay we outline the contours of the epistemolgical debates implied in the first two sections of this book. Our aim in doing so is threefold: 1) to acquaint the reader with feminist perspectives on social science, 2) to facilitate the inter-penetration of feminist ideas with critical criminological theory and research, and 3) to explore how these ideas can be brought to bear on the critical study of racism and criminal justice.

POSITIVIST EMPIRICISM

Wilbanks pursues his investigation of the NDT through a traditional positivistic approach to the production of scientific knowledge. Social scientists working from this approach assume that through strict adherence to methodological rules, they, and others like them, can and should be objective, dispassionate, value-free observers of 'natural' social life. They are trained to believe that they can prevent the political or ethical perspectives engendered by their class, race, ethnicity, gender, age, etc. from tainting their observations and interpretations of social facts. In short, they believe that the facts can and should speak for themselves.

Indeed, Wilbanks clearly asserts that through his methodology he has attained objectivity; he has allowed the facts about racism and criminal justice to speak for themselves through a technically correct, quantitative statistical analysis of officially generated data. He rejects qualitative research in general, and the personal observations and case study data of Mann and Georges-Abeyie in particular, as unscientific, subjective, and infused with bias. Thus, Wilbanks has framed his thesis and directed the

debate from the epistemological standpoint of traditional empiricism —
objectivity can be separated from subjectivity through abstract data,
quantitative methods and positivist methodology, and this separation
must occur in order for knowledge to be valid.

The epistemological basis of Wilbanks' work must be recognized in
order to recast the terms of the debate from one about competing
methods and methodology to a more accurate and fundamental one
about the validity of competing knowledge claims. Sandra Harding, a
feminist philosopher, defines *methods* as the techniques of gathering
data (listening, observing, and examining historical records),
methodology as a theory of how research is or should be done, and
epistemology as a theory of knowledge that addresses questions about
"...who can be a knower...; what tests beliefs must pass in order to be
legitimated as knowledge...; what kinds of things can be known...; the
nature of objectivity...; the appropriate relationship between the
researcher and her/his research subjects...; what should be the
purposes of the pursuit of knowledge..." (1987a:181).

This concern over 'what is worth knowing', 'who can know it' and
'how' is central to the Willbanks/Mann/Georges-Abeyie exchange.
Wilbanks rejects the knowledge claims of Mann and Georges-Abeyie
because they challenge the epistemological grounds of his argument
(articulated within the framework of the quantitative vs. qualitative
debate), their relationship to the issue (they are both 'black and
liberal') and the passionate and involved style in which they present
their evidence. He exhorts the audience to read a "more objective
review" of the book, but does not explain what makes the reviewer,
John Hagan, 'more neutral'.

Feminist critiques of positivist inquiry call its premise of objectivity
into question. They have identified at least two alternative
epistemologies — 'feminist empiricism' and 'feminist standpoint' —
that challenge the objectivity, and thus the validity, of knowldege
produced through adherence to traditional rules of method. Each of
these are represented in this volume in a general critical, rather than
specifically femininst, form as possible responses to Wilbanks and the
NDT. We discuss each in relation to their ability to rearticulate issues
relating to the present debates.

CRITICAL EMPIRICISM

Lynch (1989) recently argues that in order for the critical paradigm
to gain yardage on the playing field of academic discourse, a field
owned and operated by scholars wedded to positivist epistemology and
quantitative research methods, critical criminologists should adopt the
critical empiricist approach. Scholars working within this approach do
not reject quantitative research, but try to do it better. They argue that

the empirical model can be transformed in a way that is consistent with a critical perspective. Guided by well-constructed, class, race, ethnicity and gender conscious theory in defining problems, framing research questions, selecting data and analysis strategies, and interpreting results, researchers can conduct statistical data analysis in a manner that minimizes the biases inherent in positivist epistemology and which reveals critical insights (Lynch 1989 and Thomas and O'Maolchatha 1989).

The critical empiricist approach is well represented in this volume. The essays by Georges-Abeyie, Lynch, and Ansari identify numerous definitional, conceptual and methodological problems with Wilbanks' investigation of the NDT. Their collective critique takes Wilbanks to task for practicing 'bad empirical science' and implies that a 'good empirical science' is possible. Indeed, practicing a better empiricism is the goal of the research by Patterson and Lynch, Lynch and Patterson and DeKeseredy and MacLean in the second section of the book.

Critical empiricism, like feminist empiricism, has the potential to be subversive. By arguing for a more rigorous adherence to empirical norms, it calls these norms into question. According to Harding (1987a, 1987b), a feminist empiricism undercuts positivist assumptions by recognizing that bias is introduced by the very nature of what she terms the "context of discovery", or the socially structured location "where problematics are identified and defined" (1987b: 290). Similarly, it rejects positivist claims that the social identity of the researcher is irrelevant to the validity of the knowledge produced through scientific inquiry. Instead, feminist empiricists assume that the researcher's race, ethnicity, class and gender conditions her/his identification and definition of 'what counts' as a problem worthy of study, as well as where and how s/he looks for solutions. They urge researchers to "locate themselves in the same critical plane as their subject matters" (Harding 1987b:184) in order to open for public scrutiny the subjective viewpoint that conceives and orchestrates research activity. Acknowledging the 'subjective' stance of the researcher at once "increases the objectivity of the research and decreases the 'objectivism' which hides this kind of evidence from the public" (Harding 1987a: 9). Accordingly, researchers should articulate and defend publicly the criteria guiding their selection of problems, and their definitions of what is problematic about them, just as they publicize and defend their research methods.

The methodological critiques in this volume help to identify, challenge and remedy the Eurocentric and middle-class bias inherent in Wilbanks' work, a bias that Wilbanks himself does not recognize. Wilbanks tells us he is motivated by his concern for the legitimacy of the 'system', and he views the 'myth' of its racist nature as the source of its demise. Thus, he sets out simply to confirm the null hypothesis: there is no relationship between race and criminal justice processing. Alternatively, the critical empiricist work in this volume re-orients the questions asked (and the analysis strategies pursued) to consider what is relevant to the daily life problems of offenders from subordinated racial and ethnic groups — questions such as: "'in what forms', and 'under what conditions', does racism reflect itself in criminal justice processes?" In doing so, they provide a starting point for recentering the debate. Unfortunately, critical empiricism at its best can only begin the critical reconstruction needed to seriously address the pervasive influence of class, race and gender biases in the mainstream literature.

CRITICAL STANDPOINT

The unifying theme of this book is that of dialectical reasoning — thesis, antithesis, synthesis. Synthesis is actually the negation of the negation and thus a recreation. Similarly, feminist standpoint epistemology rejects the antithesis — critical empiricism — and claims to offer a better strategy for creating and evaluating knowledge. In contrast to critical and feminist empiricists, feminist standpoint theorists challenge the emancipatory potential of empiricist inquiry and reject it on that basis. These feminist scholars contend that the point of producing knowledge is to change the world; this endeavor requires both a new epistemology and new methodology.

Harstock (1983) locates the parentage of a feminist standpoint approach in Marxist epistemology and its emphasis on the proletarian standpoint as a privileged one which produces a truer, less distorted picture of social reality than that available to the bourgeoisie. The basis of this epistemological assumption is the materialist conception that concrete human activity structures and sets limits on understanding. Through the practical daily activity of engaged struggle against existing conditions of class domination, the oppressed class achieves a more inclusive vision of social reality. Harstock (1983) argues that a feminist materialism expands the Marxian account to consider how gender relations structure practical activity needed to achieve human emancipation, and we would argue that this idea should be expanded to include the consideration of how race relations do the same. "Racism is the incestuous child of patriarchy and capitalism now full grown" (Joseph 1981); it is folly to think that we can understand one without viewing it in relation to the others.

Consistent with Hartstock's analysis, Collins' sketch of an Afrocentric feminist standpoint epistemology provides a most insightful counterpoint to positivist epistemology. She begins by noting that:

....values and ideas that Africanist scholars identify as being characteristically "Black" often bear remarkable resemblance to similar ideas claimed by feminist scholars as being characteristically "female". This similarity suggests that the material conditions of oppression can vary dramatically and yet generate some uniformity in the epistemologies of subordinate groups (Collins 1989:756-7).

Generally, Afrocentric and feminist standpoint epistemologies share characteristics constituting them as person-centered "epistemologies of connection" in which "truth emerges through care" (Collins 1989:757). They are united in opposition to positivist epistemology which values abstract knowledge obtained through disinterested, impersonal procedures. More specifically, Collins' (1989) version of an Afrocentric feminist perspective has the following four interrelated characteristics:

1 *Concrete experience is a criterion of meaning.* Wisdom and knowledge are intimately linked to concrete personal experience. One who has not experienced oppression, either through first-hand experience or empathetic connection to the oppressed, cannot really know what it means.

2 *The use of dialogue in assessing knowledge claims.* Speaking, listening and responding are female and African-American interaction patterns that emphasize personal connection. Knowledge cannot be validated in isolation; the studier and the studied become actively engaged in the research process.

3 *Ethic of caring.* The ethic of caring is composed of three elements: 1) an emphasis on individual uniqueness, 2) the acceptance of the appropriateness of emotions in dialogues, and 3) the development of the capacity for empathy.

4 *Ethic of personal accountability.* Researchers' values cannot be separated from the product of their reseach. Inquiry always has an ethical aim; thus, social scientists must be held accountable for the ethical implications of their knowledge claims.

Collins argues that the significance of this epistemology "may lie in its enrichment of our understanding of how subordinate groups create knowledge that enables them to resist oppression" (1989:757). We agree and suggest that it could provide crucial points of connection for all critical scholars.

Mann and George-Abeyie reject Wilbanks' knowledge claims on the basis that they are incongruent with the concrete experience of subjugated groups. For them, the fruits of his labor constitute knowledge without wisdom which, in Collins' words, "is adequate for the powerful, but wisdom is essential to the survival of the subordinate" (1989:759). Wilbanks, like the critical empiricists who negate him, chooses a method that relies on abstraction, rather than concrete experience, and a methodology that rules out dialogue with the objects of the 'system' that he studies. Generously, Mann states that she can accept Wilbanks' methods and results "if and when they are buttressed by observational, ethnographic, ancedotal, and other qualititative data." Clearly, however, his epistemological position requires him to reject such a strategy as a legitimate knowledge producing activity.

Wilbanks rejects the validity of knowledge obtained via dialogue both by rejecting qualitative data as unscientific and by calling for 'those' who disagree with him to address the issues only on his terms, as defined by questions he imposes. That his work is not guided by an ethic of care is best illustrated by his foolish interpretation of his results, *i.e.*, that leniency against some minority offenders could cancel out the discriminatory treatment of others. Most importantly, Wilbanks is unconcerned with the ethical implications of his work, as revealed by his interchange with Mann regarding the inflammatory nature of his book. Rather than address the essence of Mann's concern, Wilbanks responds by calling upon her to produce studies that disconfirm his thesis.

We must point out that the methodological implications of critical standpoint epistemologies do not simply begin and end with the standard debate over quantitative *vs.* qualitative methods. The requirement of personal accountability must be understood not just in the context of what to do with findings once someone has produced them, but also in terms of the very nature of the production process itself. It shifts the terms of the debate to the *purpose* of the knowledge producing activity as an important methodological criteria that must be considered in evaluating knowledge claims. The experience of purposive participation in exposing and changing racist, classist, sexist and imperialist practices generates the 'best' knowledge and is the experience against which all other claims of knowledge must be evaluated. Viewed from this position, a standpoint is more than a perspective that can be claimed by anyone; it is an achievement (Harding, 1987a: 185).

A critical standpoint epistemology requires a social scientist to be an activist, and at the same time, to value and promote the experiences of social activists as social scientific knowledge. Not only must we root our knowledge claims in the lived experience of the people whom we are researching, but we must recognize their struggle as consistent with our own. At a minimum, this requires on-going dialogue, care and personal accountability in all knowledge producing activities. More concretely, in the context of the present debate, it means creating opportunities for individuals *and their families* to tell, and have valued as knowledge, their personal accounts of how racist, classist and sexist practices within society in general, and the criminal justice system in particular, impacts the reality of their daily lives. Unfortunately, while qualitative research from a critical standpoint is alluded to in this book, none is presented.

CONCLUSION

The publication of this volume acknowledges that as critical scholars, we cannot dismiss Wilbanks' analysis as simply false consciousness. It does fit quite nicely into the dominant belief system in this country. Therefore, we must treat it as part of the social reality that must be confronted in the struggle against racial injustice in U.S. society. Similarly, we cannot ignore Wilbanks' positivist epistemological stance and its attendant claims to a value-free research methodology, as they undermine the practical value of intellectual thought and practice.

In this essay, we have noted how both feminist/critical empiricist and feminist/critical standpoint epistemologies oppose positivist claims to objectivity. Because traditional positivists own the playing field, critical empiricism may be the necessary short-term tactic for destabilizing the foundations of these claims. However, we perceive an equally pressing practical need for an alternative conception of 'what counts' as criminological knowledge so that the debate can be reconstructed in a way that accomodates the knowledge claims of powerless groups. To that end, we have suggested that the elements of an Afrocentric feminist standpoint espistemology may serve as appropriate connecting points for all critical scholars.

More generally, the features that Harding (1987a:6-10) identifies as those characteristic of the most illuminating feminist research, may also be the features of the best research addressing racism and criminal justice. Firstly, the empirical and theoretical resources are the experiences of subjugated peoples — women and men. Research designs and conclusions that do not fit the experiential reality of the people must be rejected. Secondly, inquiry must aim to provide information *for* subjugated women and men, explanations of social reality that they want and need, rather than for those who control, pacify, exploit and manipulate. Thirdly, the public must be able to scrutinize the totality of the research project which includes the researcher's class, race, culture and gender beliefs and practices.

Making connections with feminist thought(s) implies the question: "is racism in the criminal justice system a 'feminist issue' given the small proportion of offenders who are women?" We think that it must be. Feminists must work toward bettering the lives of all women, especially those with the least power to resist the most powerful forms of oppression. Perhaps as importantly, it is time to truly escape the blinders of abstraction and recognize that in real life, male offenders do not exist as exclusive objects. They are connected in relationships with other people, a major portion of whom are women — mothers, wives, lovers, sisters and daughters. Any woman who fights to keep her wits, and her roof, about her as she helplessly experiences a loved one being swept away by the currents of criminal justice 'knows' the true brutality of the system and the extensiveness of its destruction. If she is a racial/ethnic minority person, which she is likely to be, and/or if she is poor, which she surely is, she intuitively knows the nature of the interaction between criminal justice practices and the racist and/or classist structure of her society, as well as its impact on her life, her family and her community. Mostly, as a woman, she knows that it *is* a women's issue.

REFERENCES

Ansari, Z. reference to this volume

Collins, P.H. (1989) "The Social Construction of Black Feminist Thought" *Signs: Journal of Women in Culture and Society*. 14(4):745-773.

DeKeseredy, W. and B. MacLean reference to this volume.

Georges-Abeyie, D. reference to this volume

Harding, S. (1987a) *Feminism and Methodology*. Bloomington, IN: Indiana University Press.

Harding, S. (1987b) "The Instability of Analytical Categories of Feminist Theory" S. Harding and J. F. O'Barr (eds.) *Sex and Scientific Inquiry,* Chicago: University of Chicago Press:283-302.

Hartstock, N. (1983) *Money, Sex and Power* Boston: Northeastern University Press.

Joseph, G. (1981) "The Incompatable Menage a Trois: Marxism, Feminism and Racism" L. Sargent (ed.) *Women and Revolution: A Discussion of the Unhappy Marriage of Marxism and Feminism* Boston: South End Press.

Lynch, M. J. reference to this volume

Lynch, M. J. (1989) "Critical Theory and Quantitative Analysis: Us and Them" *The Critical Criminologist.* 1(3):6.

Lynch, M. J. and E. B. Patterson reference this volume

Mann, C. R. reference to this volume

Thomas, J. and A. O'Maolchatha (1989) "Reassessing the Critical Metaphor: An Optimistic Revisionist View" *Justice Quarterly* 6(2)

CHAPTER 16

A Question of Assumptions

Marjorie S. Zatz
Arizona State University

Whether they are stated explicitly or remain implicit, assumptions form the core of all social scientific research. The fundamental assumptions underlying a research project establish the parameters within which it is conceived and executed. They inform all stages of the project, from the questions posed through the collection of data and selection of methodological approach, to the interpretation of results. Assumptions are not themselves readily amenable to empirical testing; rather, they are simply accepted because they make sense to the researcher and provide a structure for what would otherwise be chaos. For example, researchers working from a consensus paradigm assume that societal members share a basic set of values and perceptions (including who and what causes the greatest social harm) while researchers working from a conflict paradigm assume that there are power differentials within any given society and those with more power impose their views on those with less power. Most long-standing debates in criminology, as in the other social (and probably physical) sciences, can be attributed to a difference in basic assumptions. The debate over whether or not the criminal justice system is racist is no exception.

WILBANKS' ASSUMPTIONS

As Georges-Abeyie has noted, the assumptions informing Wilbanks' analysis are derived from the basic consensus perspective as refined for criminological research by Michael Hindelang (1978). These assumptions stand in opposition to the assumptions underlying the research of many of the other scholars represented in this book, including my own, which are derived from conflict or critical paradigms. Wilbanks either states or implies the following theoretical and conceptual assumptions in his book, *The Myth of a Racist Criminal Justice System*, and in his chapters included in this reader: (1) discrimination is the behavioral manifestation of a prejudicial attitude; (2) discrimination is necessarily conscious and intentional, and for a system to be called discriminatory it must be consciously designed to result in disparities; (3) discrimination is divorced from power relations — it is as possible for less powerful groups to discriminate against more powerful groups as it is for more powerful groups to discriminate against less powerful groups; and (4) the various bases for discrimination (e.g., race, ethnicity, gender, class) are distinct rather than interwoven.

These theoretical assumptions imply a related set of methodological assumptions which structure Wilbanks' analysis and conclusions: (5) the only valid evidence for or against a finding of discrimination is the presence or absence of a main effect of race; and even more specifically (6) an increasing divergence in outcomes between groups as one moves through the system (*i.e.*, a cumulative effect); and (7) to be considered discrimination, differences between groups must be evidenced by systematic and systemic disparities throughout *all* stages of the criminal justice system and across *all* jurisdictions.

LIMITATIONS OF WILBANKS' CONCEPTUAL ASSUMPTIONS

As a set, these assumptions constrain research on discrimination — be it racial, ethnic, gender, or class based — within excessively restrictive parameters. For example, they exclude evidence of informal 'petit apartheid' discussed by Georges-Abeyie and Richie Mann from the purview of discrimination. They also exclude indirect and interaction effects of race (and ethnicity, gender, and class) on court processing and sanctioning decisions, even when these effects are systematic, systemic, and statistically significant. Moreover, they establish such a rigid and restrictive framework within which it is impossible, given these assumptions, to find discrimination within contemporary liberal society — not because racism does not exist, but because Wilbanks has eliminated it by fiat.

Elsewhere, I have distinguished between overt and subtle forms of discrimination that have become institutionalized in the U.S. criminal justice system (Zatz, 1987). Basing my distinction on statistical criteria, I define *overt* discrimination as main effects (*i.e.*, statistically significant direct effects of race, gender, or other group membership after other relevant factors have been statistically held constant). By way of contrast, *subtle* forms of discrimination are evidenced by statistically significant indirect and interaction effects of group membership operating through other variables.

Based upon his essay "Reaction to McCleskey *vs* Georgia", it appears that Wilbanks would reject my thesis that subtle forms of discrimination exist, since he ridicules the concept of subtle discrimination as "a non-falsifiable thesis". Contrary to Wilbanks' assertion, the presence or absence of such subtle effects can be tested using the quantitative analytic techniques he prefers, so long as analysis is not limited to testing solely for main effects. Thus, my thesis is clearly falsifiable. The difference between our views is one of assumptions. Wilbanks assumes that main effects (what I call overt discrimination) are the only evidence of discrimination (indeed, he

Marjorie S. Zatz

takes it a step further, insisting on a consistent series of main effects), while I assume that discrimination can be overt *or* subtle in form. Thus, by my definition, institutionalized disparities, whether overt or subtle, fall within the purview of discrimination when they systematically favor one group over another.

In the DeKeseredy and MacLean article, the relevant bills probably were not intended to discriminate; however, the criteria used to assess the likelihood of success on parole are culturally specific and they systematically disadvantage Canadian Native prisoners. As Petersilia has noted, in many instances where racial disparities are found today "they seem to have developed because the system adopted procedures without analyzing their possible effects on different racial groups" (1983:112).

Whether or not an act was consciously intended to result in discrimination is critical to Wilbanks because of the importance he attaches to conscious, intentional acts resulting from a prejudicial attitude. Tied to this are his assumptions that we can identify the prejudiced person responsible for an act of discrimination, and that racism can be defined in solely psychological terms as "an evil motive or trait attributed to the 'out-group'". Indeed, in Wilbanks' critique of Baldus, he argues that we need to know the race of the specific prosecutors and jurors involved in the various cases in order to determine whether or not they "exercised racial discrimination against blacks by devaluing black life via leniency to those who killed blacks rather than whites". In the same essay, however, Wilbanks lays bare the flaw inherent in this assumption:

> Unfortunately, the decision to require proof of direct discrimination in a particular case flies in the face of prior decisions and establishes a burden that will be difficult, if not impossible, to meet. How can anyone prove that discrimination occurred in a particular case unless someone admits to making a decision based on race? This standard has not been imposed in other spheres such as in employment discrimination and jury discrimination so it is difficult to see why such a stringent standard should be applied in death penalty cases" (Wilbanks, this volume).

In this passage, he perhaps inadvertently suggests the possibility that a system could institutionalize racism even without any individually identified decision maker consciously acting upon racist beliefs.

Wilbanks' assumptions lead him to dismiss subtle forms of discrimination, including indirect effects, but he assumes that an increasing divergence in outcomes between groups as one moves through the system is necessary for us to conclude that the criminal justice system is racist. This requirement is certain not to be met, however, since as Georges-Abeyie points out, the criminal justice 'system' is really a set of interrelated yet disjointed series of processes, not a single unified system. In contrast, my distinction between the two forms of discrimination allows us to disentangle a cumulative series of main effects (*i.e.*, overt discrimination) from the cumulatively disadvantaging indirect effects of race (or gender, ethnicity, or class) that provide evidence of institutionalized subtle discrimination.

LIMITATIONS OF WILBANKS' METHODOLOGICAL ASSUMPTIONS

Wilbanks waffles on yet another assumption. In rebutting Richey Mann's critique of his work, Wilbanks states that he favors statistical analysis over observational analysis. Observational research, according to Wilbanks, is "heavily influenced by bias and racial prejudice" since "the tendency is for those with a particular bias to select that explanation which is consistent with their bias", while statistical analyses of large data sets with control variables "are a safeguard against personal bias and are far more valid as a means to 'truth'" (Wilbanks, this volume). Yet in his critique of the Baldus study, Wilbanks aims a similar accusation at statistical research, including his own, by stating "I am an ardent advocate of gun control and I know that there is a strong temptation to 'slant' my research to support my position... I am the first to admit that my position on gun control, the death penalty, etc., does influence my research".

Does Wilbanks mean that his position influences the types of questions that he asks or his interpretation of the data? Of course it does, but he seems to confuse objectivity with lack of bias. As Georges-Abeyie notes, biases are hidden in the conceptualization of research questions, and thus in the specific questions asked and not asked. To this I would add that biases are hidden in the kinds of data considered and ignored, and in the selection of methodological strategies. Characteristic of consensus-based research, Wilbanks ignores the importance of the choice of control variables (by both the researcher and the court, since most quantitative data on court processing are gathered by the courts themselves). Within the general category of quantitative statistical analysis, the researcher must decide whether to examine main effects only or to also consider interaction and indirect effects, and whether to use or ignore techniques to reduce the effects of sample selection bias. As I have concluded elsewhere, "research that tests only for main effects (*i.e.*, overt bias) and does not investigate all of the possible manifestations of discrimination may erroneously conclude that discrimination does not exist when, in fact, it does" (Zatz, 1987:83). And, research has shown that selection bias often masks discrimination (Klepper, Nagin, and Tierney, 1983; Zatz and Hagan, 1985).

Wilbanks accuses studies finding discrimination of being "marked by flaws in design or interpretation". Yet, as Ansari's contribution demonstrates, in testing his thesis Wilbanks makes a number of methodological decisions that are either incorrect or unduly limiting. To these I would add his assertion that he has controlled for sample selection bias when he has not adequately done so.

His methodological weakness is further evidenced in this volume by his remarks to Richey Mann concerning patterns and rates of offending. Richey Mann presents 1986 Uniform Crime Report data showing very similar patterns of offending for blacks, Asian Americans, Hispanics, American Indians, and whites. Wilbanks' rejoinder is appalling for its shockingly condescending and paternalistic tone, inexcusable in scholarly debate. Beyond this, his criticism is wrong. While he is certainly correct in noting the difference between rates and patterns, he improperly assumes that between-group variation is the only valid indicator of difference, thereby summarily dismissing the vast literature on comparisons of within-group variance that allow us to determine whether the same model operates for two or more subgroups. Perhaps this explains why he never examines interaction models (which would show whether or not the models for two or more subgroups differ in the direction and magnitude of the effects of other variables on an outcome), a technique that is now standard in the social sciences. Between-group effects are clearly important; but, so are comparisons of patterns within-groups, and ignoring them is a serious flaw in Wilbanks' work.

INTERSECTIONS OF RACE, ETHNICITY, GENDER, AND CLASS RELATIONS

Wilbanks further assumes that discrimination is divorced from power relations and that the various bases for discrimination are distinct rather than interwoven. These assumptions can be attributed to his more encompassing assumption that discrimination is the behavioral manifestation of a prejudicial attitude. This allows him to posit that blacks discriminate against whites more than whites discriminate against blacks — an argument that from my set of assumptions (based upon power differentials within society rather than psychological factors) is ludicrous. As Georges-Abeyie has evidenced, this is also related to Wilbanks' faulty assumption that blacks are an ethnic and economic monolith, thereby ignoring important sources of variation within the group 'blacks'. But Wilbanks is not alone in lumping all blacks, or even all non-whites, into one supposedly homogeneous grouping, as is evidenced by the Lynch and Patterson chapter in this volume. Largely due to coding decisions made by the courts, it is often impossible to distinguish between ethnic groupings in court-generated data sets, yet where such data are available research has shown differences in the court processing and sanctioning of members of different ethnic groups (e.g., Gruhl, Welch and Spohn, 1984; Hagan and Zatz, 1985; LaFree, 1985; Zatz, 1984, 1985).

As Lynch has noted, Wilbanks ignores any relationship between race (or ethnicity) and class, relegating it to a spurious or incidental connection. Yet this is a complex relationship, and to disavow any indirect or interaction effects of race and class on decision making over-simplifies both the nature of this relationship and its effects. Similarly, Wilbanks does not attend to the relationships between race and ethnicity and gender. Conversely, several studies have examined these relationships. For example, Visher (1983) and Spohn, Welch and Gruhl (1985) found that chivalry applies to white, but not non-white, women.

CONCLUSION

Wilbanks attempts to understand what is an inherently sociological phenomenon through a set of psychological assumptions. This confusion of levels of analysis is perhaps the fundamental flaw in his analysis. Discrimination cannot be reduced to a behavioral manifestation of a prejudicial attitude. So doing causes Wilbanks to dismiss as irrelevant social structural factors and history, claiming that a history of racial discrimination in a wide variety of social spheres (e.g., employment, education, housing) does not bear on the question of whether the criminal justice system discriminates. Thus, he dismisses the very structural factors that are of greatest concern to sociologists.

The assumptions underlying Wilbanks' work cause him to ignore institutionalized forms of discrimination in his search for decision-makers who will publicly acknowledge that they are acting on the basis of their prejudices. Under conditions of bourgeois liberalism, such acknowledgment would undercut the legitimacy of those individuals and of the criminal justice system as a societal institution. Ironically, we now seem to be entering an era in the United States where such acknowledgments may once again become acceptable. A few years ago, I suggested that we should not expect to see overt discrimination in contemporary U.S. criminal justice processing (Zatz, 1987). I may have been wrong. The rapid rise of racial, ethnic, and gender-based hate violence in recent years, perhaps reflecting fears by white males that they are in danger of losing their privileged position in U.S. society, may make overtly racist statements acceptable in U.S. courtrooms — a phenomenon that has not been systematically evidenced since the Civil Rights Movement; however, this would *not* imply the reappearance of discrimination. Discrimination has not gone away. Rather, it would be indicative of the reappearance of a particularly odious form of discrimination *in addition to* its other forms.

Marjorie S. Zatz

These other, more subtle, forms of discrimination have not disappeared, but instead are so fundamentally a part of our social institutions, and have become so normalized, that scholars such as Wilbanks do not even see them.

REFERENCES

Gruhl, J. S. Welch, and C. Spohn (1984) "Women as Criminal Defendants: A Test for Paternalism" *Western Political Quarterly* 37:456-467.

Hagan, J. and M.S. Zatz (1985) "The Social Organization of Criminal Justice Processing Activities" *Social Science Research* 14:103-125.

Hindelang, M. (1978) "Race and Involvement in Common Law Personal Crimes" *American Sociological Review* 43:93-109

Klepper, S., D. Nagin, and L. Tierney (1983) "Discrimination in the Criminal Justice System: A Critical Appraisal of the Literature" A. Blumstein (ed.), *Research in Sentencing: The Search for Reform, Volume II.* Washington: National Academy Press.

LaFree, G.D. (1985) "Official Reactions to Hispanic Defendants in the Southwest" *Journal of Research in Crime and Delinquency* 22:213-237.

Lizotte, A.J. (1978) "Extra legal Factors in Chicago's Criminal Courts: Testing the Conflict Model of Criminal Justice" *Social Problems* 25:564-580.

Petersilia, J. (1983) *Racial Disparities in the Criminal Justice System* Santa Monica, CA: Rand.

Spohn, C., S. Welch, and J. Gruhl (1985) "Women Defendants in Court: The Interaction Between Sex and Race in Convicting and Sentencing" *Social Science Quarterly* 66:178-185.

Visher, C.A. (1983) "Gender, Police Arrest Decisions, and Notions of Chivalry" *Criminology* 21:5-25.

Zatz, M.S. (1984) "Race, Ethnicity, and Determinate Sentencing: A New Dimension to an Old Controversy" *Criminology* 22:147-171.

Zatz, M.S. (1985) "Pleas, Priors and Prison: Racial/Ethnic Differences in Sentencing" *Social Science Research* 14:169-193.

Zatz, M.S. (1987) "The Changing Forms of Racial/Ethnic Biases in Sentencing" *Journal of Research in Crime and Delinquency* 24:69-92.

Zatz, Marjorie S. and John Hagan (1985) "Crime, Time, and Punishment: An Exploration of Selection Bias in Sentencing Research" *Journal of Quantitative Criminology* 1:103-126.

CHAPTER 17

CONCLUSION

Discrimination and Criminal Justice

Brian D. MacLean / Dragan Milovanovic

The essays in this book have helped to demonstrate that to de-construct the race, gender and class effects of criminal justice processing requires a confrontation with penetrating epistemological and methodological questions. Empirically oriented research devoid of theory is as one-sided in its approach as theoretical investigations which are not grounded empirically. Together, research and theory form a dialectic unity — both inform each other. In terms of research, we have seen that all methods — whether quantitative or qualitative — have strengths *and* limitations, and that the wise researcher is cognizant of those particular limitations when drawing conclusions from the investigation. Due to such limitations, a combination of research methods is most desirable. Thus, qualitative research methods should be used in combination with quantitative methods in de-constructing biases at different levels of criminal justice decision making. Whether one investigates the institutional or systematic discrimination of various 'clients' of the criminal justice system or whether one is more interested in examining more covert or hidden forms of discrimination, the most valid findings are those which are corroborated by a number of research techniques.

In this collection of essays, we have seen that definitional issues remain unresolved. For example, how is it that we operationally define 'racism', 'covert biases'and 'institutional biases'? If Wilbanks has made a contribution to social scientific research, it has been in providing an articulate yet simply stated position. Although quite controversial, his position must be debated and refuted, not by fiat, but by reasoned analyses which consider all forms of data.

Accordingly, the essays presented here have addressed the NDT at different levels of analysis. It has been argued that positivistic methodologies are suspect. Those rooted in the consensus paradigm are particularly suspect because they often reflect a phallocentric bias and while appearing objective, these methodologies are constructed upon race, gender, and class-based value positions. Unresolved is the question of whether positivistic empiricism is, in fact, inherently biased — whether employed by the Left or the Right. A critical empiricist approach such as the one advocated by Lynch, Zatz, Georges-Abeyie, and Ansari certainly provides the conceptual tools necessary for de-construction and the development of broader insights into more subtle processes of discrimination in the social formation. Danner, Landis, and Zatz have argued that in its stance against positivistic assumptions, feminist empiricism is also inherently subversive, particularly by stipulating that the social identity of the researcher is a relevant variable in scientific inquiry. As Danner and Landis point out, researchers should not only defend their research methodologies, but they must also articulate their value stance and defend it openly. In particular, questions of criteria and assumptions that may guide the selection of the problem at hand and what indeed is problematic about it must be raised and properly evaluated.

Advocates of the discrimination thesis have argued throughout this volume that discrimination exists at many levels, and hence must be studied with a methodology sensitive to this reality. For example, as French argues, racism can be institutionalized by governmentally funded programs that claim to be doing the opposite. At the other end, 'petit apartheid' is omnipresent. There is little doubt that its effects are cumulative. This short book has been an exercise in a critical examination of race, gender, and class biases in the criminal justice system. It only begins to articulate the magnitude of discrimination. In many ways it has been more of a pedagogical tool for sensitizing critical readers to approaches in examining the problem than a simplistic formula for solution.

In closing, however, some of the ambivalence expressed by Headley is shared by us in undertaking this anthology:

> *proposing the nonexistence of racism in the criminal justice system is intended, at least so it seems to me, to goad us into a distracting sideshow, to divert our attention from the larger social reality which produces the human wreckage...in which the justice system serves as custodian.*